Life: Traveling with Gusto

Don's Story

Life: Traveling with Gusto
Don's Story

D. K. Heichel

WestBow
PRESS
A DIVISION OF THOMAS NELSON

ISBN: 978-1-4497-5265-1 (sc)
ISBN: 978-1-4497-5264-4 (e)

Library of Congress Control Number: 2012908863

WestBow Press books may be ordered through booksellers or by contacting:

WestBow Press
A Division of Thomas Nelson
1663 Liberty Drive
Bloomington, IN 47403
www.westbowpress.com
1-(866) 928-1240

Scripture taken from the King James Version of the Bible.

Printed in the United States of America

WestBow Press rev. date: 03/05/2013

To Don

I know the thoughts that I think toward you, saith the Lord, thoughts of peace, and not of evil, to give you an expected end. Jeremiah 29:11

Table of Contents

List of Illustrations

Preface

Life: Traveling with Gusto is about faith, grief, and God's unending mercy. I found God to be a loving, and caring father who wants the best for us. Through tragedy, he loved me and cared for me. I want to tell the story how I lost faith and found it again.

In the process, I learned about myself, grief, and strength. We may lose people we love, our homes, friendships and pets. In addition we may also be diagnosed with illness. If we live long enough, we know tragedy strikes.

We find strength in God's love, mercy and compassion. We know God is with us. He is our backbone when life gets tough. We lean on him to bring us through troubles. He does not always answer our prayers the way we want however as older people say, He is always on time.

I thought about many scriptures as I wrote. These scriptures pertain to marriage, God's unending love and forgiveness. They were my source of help. You will notice each chapter begins with a verse because they relate to the circumstances or situation. I found the Bible especially Psalm described my feelings. I hope these will help you as well. I use the King James Version throughout because it is public domain. However, other translations may be easier to read. So, I encourage you to compare and read others as your walk of faith continues.

Finally I listed different resources pertaining to our experiences. These may be helpful if you know someone traveling down our road. I hope you enjoy this book. May God bless you.

Acknowledgments

First of all to God who loves me because Jesus died for my sins many years ago. God is my source of strength. I am happy to know Him.

Next, I want to thank Pat Walker for being there and being my cheering section throughout the entire process of grief and writing this book.

The wonderful staff and volunteers at Davis Hospice for helping me cope with Don's illness and death. They tended to Don as if he was their only patient. I will always be grateful for them.

Dr. Sandra Guidry and the Infusion Clinic nurses who cared for Don an entire year. Their wisdom and loving care helped him live the quality of life he needed.

Dr. Thomas Cassidy who is one of the most caring physicians I have ever known.

Chaplain Delbert Hansen and Mrs. Hansen whom Without their advice before our wedding, during our marriage, and at Don's home going, we would have not survived.

Bob and Linda Thompkins' constant friendship before and after his death.

Dave and Pat Heichel for making me feel welcomed, loved and part of the family.

Finally to local Cheyenne and Loveland businesses: Marv's Other Place, Jolly Rogers RV, Schrader Funeral Home and, King GMC of Loveland for their generosity and caring.

Chapter One

Introduction

Likewise the Spirit also helpeth our infirmities: for we know not what we should pray for as we ought: the Spirit maketh intercessions for us with groanings that cannot be uttered. Romans 8:26 (KJV)

This book is about love, loving others, and accepting our lots in life though we may not want to accept the outcome. It is also about circumstances surrounding Don's diagnosis, illness, death and living life to the full as God intended. Finally, we look at grief and rising past it. Through the mayhem we enjoyed life and each other. With the help of God we survived until the end. I hope this book will be an inspiration to those who lost loved ones or other important persons. In addition I also hope it encourages those of you who have grieved or have not experienced grief yet to find closure and peace.

Donald Walter Heichel loved life. In the grand scheme of the world, he was an ordinary man. He did not have riches or fame. In fact he was just one of thousands who died from pancreatic cancer. I thought Don was not an actor or someone famous, yet, his story was important. As months passed I reflected on his life— it was wonderful. So, this story is about how he lived and gave to our community, not out of selfishness, but out of love of people.

Don was and will always remain in the memories of everyone who came into contact with him. He inspired a legacy without knowing it. Therefore the book did not start with grief it started with the beginning of Don's life and slowly worked toward grief.

As I wrote, I remembered working as a nursing assistant in the hospice and cancer center at Presbyterian Hospital, Charlotte, North Carolina. I understood cancer from a nursing assistant's point of view. I remembered standing outside patients' rooms crying because of the pain I felt for the patient and their families. However I did not really understand the family members' emotions. Sure, I read information provided by the facility about hospice. I knew about it. After all, working in the hospice unit for five years yielded many opportunities to prove my knowledge, skill, and compassion.

Now more than twenty-five years later I had a different outlook of death because now the patient was my husband. This was like a nightmare. I saw the end progress in slow motion. Intellectually, I understood the implications of cancer and the prognosis. Cancer was personal. This was not another day at the office where I distanced myself to protect myself from getting hurt. Personal meant trying to make sense of cancer and adapting any way I could. It also meant prayer, though there were plenty of times I could not reach to the Lord and pray. Those were the times the Holy Spirit interceded[1] for me and others took on the role of prayer.

It takes usually horrific circumstances to make one reflect on life. Up to this point I had weathered many bad moments. As I looked back these moments were when God intervened however, to my recollection, none of them were like this. Yes, I survived the deaths of my mother, sister, and father however Don's illness and death held more meaning.

Fourteen months of living with Don made me realize God was in complete control. Our lives changed — not because we wanted it to but because this was God's will. God had the final say we did not. We made plans however those plans were not necessarily what God wanted.[2] Therefore our situation forced us to appreciate each day. Each day was a different negative or positive experience— depending on the way we looked at it. We were together. The emotional and physical demands began taking their tolls. Each day challenged us. We began surviving, not living.

I thought I was strong enough to handle circumstances that came my way. After all I survived basic training, Security Forces Police Academy, domestic abuse, assault, child birth, and several bad marriages. However, this circumstance was more life altering than any of those unpleasant and hurtful challenges I had ever faced during my life. Yet, this experience changed my life completely.

Impending death has a way of changing one's experience level. In fact, I think how we cope with hardship says a lot about our character. Harder times usually prompts more frequent prayer. When life is good, we forget God exist. In this case, neither of us did the latter much.

Therefore, we found we had more conversations about God. How could we not have those conversations? When we know we or someone close are dying, I believe, those are times we acknowledge the power of God. What other choice do we have? I realized we were very vulnerable and dependent on God no matter how this turned out. His power was greater than ours.

At the start Don's days started well. Later, Don often remarked, "I have more bad days than good days." The bad days got progressively worse. Each of us dealt with those days knowing the end but not wanting to accept it. Our days, like a movie, played out in front of our eyes. Our characters lived out a bad to worse script. I found the prince but the prince slipped away. At the end of the love story, he died and heroine was left alone. The movie ended without the happy ever after ending. Nothing made it better, not good thoughts or possessions.

While Don faced death he also gained many material possessions however, no matter how much he accumulated death was a moment away. It was only a matter of time. That said, we cannot take any possessions with us when we die. Job said he came into this world with nothing and nothing we returned into the earth.[3] Don wanted everything he owned close to him. I moved all items in the storage locker filling the garage and shop to the rafters. I understood his reasoning— the storage facility raised its rates when the new couple began managing it.

No, it did not make sense to pay storage fees when we had enough room in the garage. However, I felt like this was a comfort to him. These treasures represented twenty-five years of marriage to his last wife and sixty-three years of his life on earth. They were his heart. In the end, those possessions remained on earth.[4]

March, April, May and June 2010 ushered in many kinds of challenges, laughter, pain and disappointment. I felt as if I was going to explode at times. No one knew how I really felt but the Lord. Days ran into days. Slept but did not sleep and caring for children and for Don. Sometimes, I did not have any strength for myself Don or anything else. So often through these months, I noticed the weather, but I did not notice it. Mostly, I noticed Don— everything about him. I noticed his moods, body language, anguish, and his beautiful eyes.

It must be an awful feeling to know one is dying. We cannot control the hour or circumstances in which it occurs. I believe Don also realized it as well. Reality hits us in the face at times during our lives. So we went into these three months with high expectations though often not real ones.

We cried to God many times beginning in March 2010 until the end. God was there. He guided us and those around us. This is a story about love, faith, a man and his life. We see joy, pain, and sorrow. So often, facing circumstances define who we are by how we handle them. Circumstances define who we eventually become. Thus, we realized without God as the center of our lives we were nothing.

Life inter-connects in many ways and it is those ways that changes us. Is it by design or did we do something to make these events happen? The Bible says, "God directs our steps." Proverbs 19:21 (KJV). It is God's will that our lives take different paths.

As this story unfolds, you will see how lives intertwined in meetings that last a lifetime. I will never forget the times we had or how we met. In the end, this meeting changed my life. It tested my faith in God. Yet through it all God never left my side though occasionally I left His. I had to find out who I was and realign my values. I will always be grateful for my experience yet part of my heart will always be empty.

Chapter Two
The Beginning

A time to love and a time to hate; a time for war, and a time for peace. Ecclesiastes 3:8 (KJV)

As I said before, God does not do anything without purpose. He knew who He wanted our parents to be. He knew when we were to be born. God decided where we were going to live and every detail about our lives. For they were written before we were conceived. God, in his infinite wisdom, allowed us to live our lives and make choices. Psalm 25:12(KJV)

In 1880, thirteen to twenty-three Heichel families lived in Ohio. Don's family was one of those families although they did not always live in Ohio. The family started in Pennsylvania.

Don's great-great-great grandfather Michael Heichel was born in 1793 in Lancaster County, Pennsylvania where he met and married Anna Catherine Albert March 4, 1819. Then the family moved from Lancaster to Middleton County, Pennsylvania. Joseph Heichel, their only child, was born November 5, 1819. Finally Mr. and Mrs. Heichel moved to Ashland County, Ohio sometime after the birth of Joseph. Some years after moving to Ohio, Michael died May 30, 1854 then Catherine died March 4, 1870.

Their son Joseph, Don's great-great grandfather married Ann Rebecca Basford. One son was born to the couple Francis Marion, February 10, 1846 in Ashland County. Francis married Rache Settie Coleman December 27, 1894 in Mansfield, Ohio. They had several children: James Earl July 8, 1898; William Orley February 20, 1900; Gladys Noama July 8, 1902; Harvey Clayton February 25, 1906; and Elmer Edward November 11, 1908. Francis died February 27, 1912 and Rache died October 7, 1942.

William wed Pauline Elizabeth King Heichel July 9, 1921. William and Pauline had three children— William Elmer January 1, 1922; Robert Glen October 18, 1923; and Dorothy M. William became Don's grandfather.

Robert married Dorothy Mae Farst July 3, 1946. Robert and Dorothy had four children: Baby Heichel passed away at birth; Donald, Dan, and David. All children were born about two years apart. Don's mother was a homemaker and his father worked for Mansfield Tire and Rubber Company which was one of the leading manufacturers during this time.[5]

Then the family lived at 229 East Second Street which runs east to west and lies between Glenn Ave and Bentley not far from downtown Mansfield. The house they resided in was a white wooden two story built in 1900 with three bedrooms and two bathrooms. It had very large windows and wooden floors. The rooms were very large as was usual for houses of that era. This house was about four years old when the family moved in. Mansfield had a low crime rate and everyone knew everyone. It was an ideal place and time to raise a family. The Heichel family grew quickly. Donald Walter Heichel made his way into the world Wednesday, May 7, 1947.

Many events characterized 1947 like discovering the Dead Sea scrolls. Government partitioned Palestine into two sections. The Videorama, a television, by Stewart-Warner, emerged. The New York Yankees won the World Series and the NFL champions were the Chicago Cardinals. Harry Truman was president. Vice presidents did not exist. Life expectancy was sixty-two point nine years. (Don lived to be sixty-three.) A new house cost about $6,650.00; a new car cost $1,290.00 and postal customers paid three cents for stamps. Gasoline pumped at fifteen cents a gallon and a breakfast at home cost less than one dollar fifteen cents.[6]

While Don's dad loved Mansfield he itched for the west. So, Robert and his friend, Walt Henry hitched rides through Cheyenne just before World War II. These two young men wanted to stay however after much debate they hitched home to Ohio. Robert left a place he loved— Cheyenne. Robert vowed to return. He later did.

Don passed to the third grade the summer of 1955. The Heichel family planned vacation. The family drove more than 1300 miles in a station wagon to reach Cheyenne, Wyoming. Don and his family stayed in a motel at the edge of the city. In those days the edge of the city was country because Cheyenne had not yet matured.

Don stood outside the motel looking at sunset with a thoughtful look on his face.

Dorothy Heichel asked her tall blond headed boy, "Don, What are you thinking?"

Don replied, "Mom I'm gonna live here one day." Don never forgot he wore a tee shirt from Cheyenne for his class picture.

Don grew up to be a tall, lanky young man with green eyes and blond hair. He was not particularly handsome, but he had spirit and an endearing quality about him that projected honesty, stubbornness, sincerity, and mischief. For instance, Don told Dorothy he was going to school. He asked her to prepare a lunch for him which she did. Don and his two cousins went hunting that day and returned home as if they went to school. They repeated these days twice more before his mother found out Don skipped school to hunt. There was another time at a family dinner when a cousin asked Don to pass the meatballs. Don passed the meatballs by putting a glob of them into her waiting hand.

During his high school years, Don was an average student but he liked football. Football was not his passion however he was good at it. Don found out the coach did not choose him to play ball the next year. Don quit the team during his junior year. He never played football again.

June 1965 Don officially graduated from Clear Forks High School at a time when young women wore dresses and heels and young men wore suits for graduation. With high school behind him, he wanted to go to college.

However, Vietnam interrupted his plans. Unlike some men during the 60's Don did not mind going to war even if Vietnam was a dreaded war. In fact, Vietnam started two years before Don was born. In 1950 America sent over 15 million dollars to the French military. By 1965, we had sent over 200,000 troops to fight.[7] Therefore, like his father, Robert, before him who proudly served in World War II Donald Walter Heichel did his part as well. He immediately answered the call. Don did not wait to be drafted. He decided to enlist. Don told me, he wanted to serve. Don signed his selective service card—33-103-47-412—May 1967, two years after graduation.

One of the proudest moments for all veterans was taking the oath proudly defending our country on foreign or domestic soil. Prospective inductees stood facing the United States flag. The heart swollen with pride we repeated our oath with right hand raised. At that moment an un-describable feeling washed over the inductee like an unending wave of warm water. We said we would give our very lives, if needed, to defend the country of our birth. At once we became part of something bigger than us. We were no longer teenagers going off to war. We were now men and women who sacrificed family, friends, and self for the freedoms we have and for our country.

We spiritually joined with those who fought before us and who will come after us. In an instant we became part of a brotherhood of individuals who unselfishly took the same oath. It did not matter how long the person wore the uniform or assigned job. It is only important that they did their part and served. We are veterans of Korea, World

War I and II, Vietnam, the cold war era, peace time, and present day conflicts. We stood and continued to stand proud and strong.

Serving in the military was and is an honor and privilege we do not take lightly. It is one of the freedoms that made our country what it is. Throughout the years so many Soldiers, Airmen, Sailors, and Marines answered the call of duty preserving our way of life. America stands on these sacrifices of many before and after Don who will fight or have fought to the death.

As members of this elite group, most of us did not pick our jobs, the military placed us where we did the most good. Some were clerks, others pilots, while others supported the home team. Each job had its place and played an important role to accomplish the mission.

The military offered young women and men the chance to see the world especially those who could not afford to travel. Don traveled. He went to Missouri, Korea, Germany, Georgia, and other points as the military saw fit.

Service also introduced us to different sins. For instance, if the person did not smoke or curse or have other vices, chances were good they developed unhealthy and ungodly habits. I do not know what vices Don picked up while he served. We never discussed it.

Finally, the military made us grow up fast. When we swore in our life lessons began. We entered service inexperienced and afraid. By time the military discharged us, we had grown mentally and physically, but maybe not spiritually.

Developing spiritually was the hardest part especially if it was not part of home life. Don said, his parents did not go to church. So entering service brought challenges he had never faced. The spiritual would come later in life, much later. For some, learning the will of God comes fast, for others it is a very, very slow process.

Earlier I said the military placed us where they needed us. They did. By all accounts, Don did not want to be a clerk. He wanted to jump from airplanes. He wanted to be an Airborne Ranger. In fact, we sang one cadence that said: "I want to be an airborne ranger!" That was Don. Don would not see action of Vietnam like so many of his comrades. The Army stationed him in Korea. The Army needed him there.

Every good military member knows two concepts, we do not question orders, and we do not assume anything. We do as told and like it. They tell us how high to jump and we jump, no questions asked. During a maneuver, Don jumped a ditch to get to the other side. (No chicken jokes please.) As he jumped he landed and broke his left ankle. Medics cut off his boot. However, his boot probably helped. The Army evacuated him to Landstule Military Hospital, Germany then stateside. Don stayed in the hospital for one year before release.

Any time the military releases us from active duty, they pay our way from the duty station to our home of record (HOR). Don's home of record was Road three, Bellville, Ohio. May 3, 1968, Specialist Donald Walter Heichel was a veteran and home for good.

Don age 7

Chapter Three
Judy Number One

Husbands, love your wives, even as Christ loved the Church, and gave his self for it. Ephesians 5:25 (KJV)

Paul tells us husbands must love their wives more than themselves. This type of love sustains, nurtures, and is passionate. God tells us not to leave each other once married. [8]However, at times situations arise making us leave the person we chose. Sometimes circumstances happen. Two people who once where so madly in love fall out of love. As a result, love grows cold or one partner may still be in love while the other falls out of love.

I found, through my life experiences that relationships take time and effort. Marriage is not a 90/10 relationship. Each person gives 100 percent or nothing. I am not saying that each person gives one hundred percent all the time. That is impossible. What I am saying is, we work at marriage. I found that each person takes ownership of their faults and tries to be there for their mate.

I am, by no means an expert on marriage. However, after marrying several times, one accepts these concepts:

first, all marriages are different and second, we all go through different phases in our lives. As we mature, we grow and change by our experiences and results of these experiences.

When we were younger, we played ball, stayed outside until dark, pretended to marry and played house. We had no idea of what marriage was really like because we viewed it with childlike innocence. Our concept of love was the same as our play. We knew we loved our parents, siblings, relatives and friends. However, as we grew older we experienced a more mature form of love.

While teens, Don nor his brothers rarely dated. Their grandfather teased them unmercifully for dating. To avoid teasing they simply did not entertain the thought of girlfriends. After all, puppy love was not real so why risk embarrassment and maybe failure? However, thoughts of dating changed when Don came back from the military. Don turned twenty-three. He was ready to settle down and have a family.

The villages of Bellville, Mansfield and surrounding areas were small. Everyone either grew up with each other or knew of each other through families and friends. Unfortunately that meant gossip. In 1970, Mansfield, Bellville, Butler and other towns were less populated than they are now, so everyone was neighbors or kin.

Don fell in love with Judy Eileen Tissot. They dated for a while and married January 10, 1970 in a little painted white church with a small steeple attached to the top and large windows that looked like a picture from a calendar. It sat back from the road a bit on a little plot of land just large enough for members to congregate after service.

When couples commit, they tell God, they are committing to Him. He is the center of the relationship. Newlywed couples have high expectations—mainly their marriage will last as long as they live; they will have two point three children, a dog and a house. They also pledge to get through good times and tough times with only death separating them.

Like many other young couples hoping for a solid relationship, Don and Judy bought a home. They settled down at RFD Two, Woodberry Road Bellville. A year later September 5, 1971, Robert (Robbie) Virgil Heichel entered Ohio at 1:45 a.m. Don was 24 and Judy 21. James (Jim) Edward Heichel came July 11, 1972 at 9:29 a.m. The small family moved to 167½ West Main Street, Lexington. These were happy times that did not last.

Children born to a marriage is not always a sign of a healthy relationship. Don and Judy's relationship began dying when these boys were eight and seven respectively. Suddenly, their world turned upside down. Dad moved out of the house and mom filed for divorce.

Divorce was a dirty word for these youngsters. Rob and Jim, the object of attention, lost a parent. They did not have a say in the break-up. Now, instead of spending Christmas with both parents they rotated around a schedule. Children spent Christmas with this parent this year and the other parent the next year. The offending parent no longer participated in their lives nor paid attention to his children.

Like adults, children go through depression, too so I am sure Judy explained divorce. In those days, divorce was not as common as it is today. These children had a stigma attached to them. Their male role model left. They depended on other men to help them become men. Child support came and went like the wind. Jim and Rob suffered. The court finalized their divorce July 11, 1980.

Don admitted to me, in those days he was not a good father or husband. In fact, he told me he was mean. Don's lack of commitment and faithfulness during his marriage ruined his relationship with his sons. Yet he was a good police officer and police chief.

Chapter Four
Police Officer Heichel

Let every soul be subject unto the higher powers.
Romans 13:1 (KJV)

Law enforcement officers are special people called to protect and serve their country, state and local communities. These fine men and women are another brotherhood, like military members risking everything defending our safety and preventing crimes. They give unselfish devotion to serving others. This occupation is a calling requiring special skills to perform a job. We do this without hesitation or concern for our welfare. I always heard, once a police officer, always a police officer. This statement rang true and later materialized again during Don's life.

Don worked at the local General Motors plant. He admitted he made good money but was not happy. He quit and pursued his dream—law enforcement. Pay was less than the plant but he loved his job. Don graduated from Ashland Police Academy May 17, 1976. Two days after that he also graduated from Basic Law

Enforcement Training (BLET) May 19, 1976 and received his badge.

When an officer graduates from the police academy, it is like swearing into the military. Graduating is an accomplishment because for weeks prior to graduation, cadets process much information all of it aimed at saving the cadet's life or the life of another person or preventing crimes. It is an honor to finish and attach the shiny new badge to the uniform.

Law enforcement required constant training to be proficient. Don knew this. July 19, 1979 and November 19, 1979 Don finished two courses given by the Ohio State Patrol. The first one was Criminal Complaint and the second was Apprehension and Prosecution.

Don was a handsome man in uniform. His size ten shoes filled 5 feet 10 inches of officer. He wore a blue uniform with a name tag that read: D.W. Heichel. His family remarked he was much taller in uniform than out.

By all accounts he did his job well and most everyone liked him. April 1979, the town council selected Don as Butler Police Chief. Letters written by the Mayors of Butler and Mansfield indicated Don was a professional. He helped change the public's view of police because Don put 100 percent of his heart into his job. He loved what he did and it showed through his dedication, and valor. Don was the type of officer many towns or cities wanted. His demeanor and unselfishness carried over from his military days to his civilian job.

Don told me of two incidences. The first one involved recovering the body of a young man. Don said one of the worst feelings he had involved diving for this unknown person. They guessed the boy died because he did not surface above the water. He and fellow officers dived long hours until they found him. Don said he felt sick.

The next time was while on patrol. One day just before school ended, several teenagers toilet papered a yard. He said he knew them and their parents. They hid when they saw him drive up. He called each child by name. The teens had two choices— clean up the yard or he told parents. These teens showed up the next day and cleaned the yard.

Don showed compassion and caring in these two situations and more. This was the type officer he was. November 1979, eight months after taking the job of chief, Don resigned. When he resigned, the Village of Butler lost a good officer. Don needed to move on to another job. He shared part of these reasons with me which I will not share. The other reasons he kept private.

Don never forgot his tour as police chief, search and rescue, volunteer fireman, patrolman, or deputy sheriff. He kept all badges and patches. When he spoke of these memories, a gleam shone in his eyes and his face brightened. He loved helping people and it showed.

Don's police badge

Chapter Five
Judy Number Two

For whither thou goest, I will go; and where thou lodgest, I will lodge. Ruth 1:16(KJV)

There are advantages and disadvantages of living in small towns. One advantage is everyone knows everyone while a disadvantage is everyone knows everyone's business. He married Alverna May 15, 1982, which only lasted about a year. The couple divorced September 2, 1983. I am certain a story existed between Don, Alverna and Judy number Two. Don married for a third time, this time to Judy number Two. Don and Judy married October 7, 1983 about a month after his divorce from Alverna.

Shortly after marriage, the State of Ohio employed Don as a State Park Ranger. The park stretched miles around with picture perfect scenery. Camping areas, green grass and plenty of trees invited visitors from all over to stay. The sparkling water accepted small and large water craft. Camp grounds were plentiful and park visitors enjoyed all it had to offer.

However, his new wife wanted to leave Ohio. Don loved this job and hated to leave it though said he wanted to remain in one place, they moved. Judy found a campground available for purchase. They moved to Indiana to buy it. However, after moving, the couple found that the deal was not financially sound. The old saying goes if it is too good to be true, then it probably is stood. That was the case with this venture. The thrill of self-employment appealed to the couple. However, they soon became embattled in a legal case. They lost the campground.

Don was never one to give up easily so the couple moved again, this time to Missouri. Don soon landed a job at Jefferson Proving Ground as a security guard. He loved this job, too. Yet again, Don said Judy wanted to move. He quit his job. They moved to Kimmberling City, Missouri. Don and Judy worked in a restaurant there however lightening hit the restaurant and destroyed it. Don and Judy managed property upon completion of the new restaurant. Again, because of circumstances Don found another job as a security guard at Silver Dollar City near Branson. Now he worked two part time seasonal jobs.

At the end of the season, the couple moved again this time to Loveland Colorado. One situation or the other arose time and time again. Don usually worked for several companies at once. If it was not one thing it was something else during a span of about three years. Basically all of these jobs ended suddenly for some reason just as they did in previous locations.

He got another job at Wilderness America in Estes Park, Colorado. Unfortunately, the manager and his wife got into a disagreement with Judy and Don. Since they co-managed the property he had to quit. Instead of sitting back and waiting for a handout, Don found yet another job at Big Thompson Motel. He and Judy again, co-managed the property along with another couple. Again, owners terminated them because the owners had too many people on staff.

Then Don and Judy had another opportunity this time to manage the LaQuinta Inn in Cheyenne. It was a good decision so they moved. As before, the company decided to release them and hire single managers so they were out of a good job once more.

Tired and disgusted, they moved again, this time to Mesa, Arizona to manage a unit for Storage USA. The position offered Judy the chance to manage the front counter and Don to perform maintenance. However as time would tell, they were again out of another job.

The couple moved back to Cheyenne. After some time they purchased Daylight Donuts. Don always wanted to work for himself. In fact he said, "This was what we worked for since leaving Ohio." The donut shop was not a large place. It was attached to two other businesses and stood on the corner of Lincolnway and another Street in Cheyenne. The little shop was not fancy by any means. It had a place of about six brown tables and chairs arranged for space and not comfort leaving a center aisle. Patrons sat and enjoyed donuts and coffee while reading the newspaper or other print media or they just visited. Walls made of paneling reminded one of an era gone by where it was more prudent to panel than paint. A small counter sat at the front of the store. Don, Judy and the part-time helper served patrons as they walked into the shop. A tall large glass display case showcasing freshly made donuts sat to the right of the cash register. Finally, the back of the store slightly seen from the cash register housed baking equipment.

Don enjoyed his work and he constantly gave back to the community donating donuts to different charities rather than throwing food in the garbage. People depended on him and he did not let them down.

He worked so hard. He told me that they did not make a lot of money. In fact they barely broke even which was just enough to pay their help, purchase supplies, pay the shop rent and cover household expenses but it was theirs. Don and Judy achieved the "American Dream" a business and home.

Sadly this ended after about a year because of Judy's diagnosis of Bakers Asthma.[9] Bakers Asthma is a form of Asthma that occurs only when around yeast and flour. Her illness forced them to sell.

So with that business gone, it was time to move onto another job. Don never gave up. He continued to strive for better. I believe his determination described the type of man he was. He found a job at River Bend Nursery which did not last long. Then he decided to go back to school this time to learn to drive tractor trailers. Immediately after graduation, Greyhound Bus Lines hired Don as a driver.

When Greyhound hired Don, two basic national lines existed—Trailways and Greyhound. At times they shared the same bus depot though in some cities there were separate depots for each line. Greyhound and Trailways serviced mostly poor to middle class people. Airline tickets cost more than two months' salary in those days, so, most riders afforded the $50.00 or less special promotion of one way to go anyplace in the lower forty-eight states deal.

Greyhound and its rival Trailways stopped in just about every small town along the way unless riders purchased express tickets. Express tickets meant buses bypassed smaller towns and drove straight through to their intended destination which was good for passengers because some bus stations shared several characteristics, noise, food and trash.

These buses were large, long vehicles painted silver or gray with a large Greyhound painted on each side. Inside two rows extended the length of the vehicle. Fabric covered seats in each row created a small center aisle. Above each row were overhead bins for small items or pieces of luggage. The under carriage held large compartments for larger parcels, suitcases or any items shipped by the line.

Bus drivers proudly glided their buses into their holding places at the depot. Upon arrival drivers most always opened the door and disembarked. Drivers stood tall and proud looking crisp and clean in grey sharply creased shirts, matching trousers, shiny shoes, black dress socks, captain hats, and attached name badges. Passengers descended the two or three steps onto waiting sidewalks as an overhead voice on the loud speaker (I thought it always sounded like the same person) clearly pronounced departure and arrival information.

As passengers, we knew these modern pieces of transportation arrived half way on time and in one piece most of the time. Drivers drove tireless all night and many hours of the day to make sure their charges arrived safely. Don's drove the Cheyenne to Omaha route which was shorter than some. However at times, he drove through Chicago which I found out later. He worked about a year spending more time in hotels than driving.

He longed for the comforts of home. So once again, he hung up his hat and found a new job in Cheyenne managing Quality Inn off of Interstate 25 North. By Heichel standards it was a step up. The couple secured a pay raise and a good job which made Don happy. Don loved this job he loved everything about it like meeting people and making his guests comfortable. However, company let Don and Judy let go when company policies changed. Don told me he was tired of moving and wanted a place to call home. However, he wanted to please his wife, so he would have gone anyplace as long as they were together.

They moved again, this time back to Estes Park, Colorado. Another opportunity came along. In 1990, they found a job managing a little hotel there called Kings Court. Another move meant more adjustments and stress which meant they worked harder at their relationship. Like previous times Judy and Don went through many hard times and good times always meeting challenges head on and not giving up.

Don often talked about his relationship with Judy so he wanted me to see where they worked and lived. We drove to see Estes Park. Don showed me motels they managed and talked about his experience working there. He told me about the last move they made from Loveland to Estes Park to Wyoming.

Estes Park looked like a picture on a post card. Mountains towered up and around this small town. Houses sat along winding roads and mountain streams. Wild animals walked in the streets like people. It was a place one reflected on God's handy-work and wonder.

Don lived the verse in the beginning to the fullest— he went where Judy went and she went where he went. He made the best of each situation and never stopped proving he loved her. As marriages go, they weathered some strong storms mainly employment, family and constant moves. Now they faced a new challenge.

Chapter Six
Why Me Lord?

My flesh and heart faileth; buy God is the strength of my heart, and my portion forever. Psalm 73:26 (KJV)

As I said before some of life's situations demand more strength than others. Yet, we find strength in God's love, mercy and compassion. [10]We know God is with us. He is our backbone when life gets tough. We lean on Him and He brings us through troubles. He does not always answer our prayers the way we want however as older people say, He is always on time.

At forty, Don told me, he and Judy were baptized in a little church in Versailles, Indiana called Shelby Christian Church. He said he felt like life was empty. I believe his belief in God helped him get through this next period of uncertainty. Don counted on God because of his faithfulness.[11]

Don went through so much some Christians would have bolted and left God in despair. Yet, Don had faith of a mustard seed even through insurmountable odds.[12]

He was down but never out as he waited for the Lord to come to his aid. God did.

In 1990, about a year into managing a motel called Kings Court in Loveland, Colorado doctors diagnosed with Don Colon cancer. Colon cancer can be a nasty cancer. Its survival rate, based on five years, is more than 70 percent depending on the patient, treatment options and stage when found.[13]

Colon cancer affects the lining of the large intestines. Family history predisposed Don. After all, his mother and father had cancer they died. Symptoms triggered an alert. His doctor, a gentle, very petite woman named Dr. Kline, based at the Veterans Administration Hospital in Denver, treated him with a year of chemotherapy and surgery to remove a large portion of his colon causing Don to have a semi-permanent colostomy[14] for a while. However doctors later reversed the procedure. Don and Judy celebrated. Don was cancer free. He appeared buff, lean and happy at the end of his year-long cancer treatment.

Life went well until three years later when Don and Judy (Number Two) found out he needed a left hip replacement. Life was downhill from there. These notes summarized medical logs captured his treatments.[15]

- November 6, 2003: Don entered the hospital for left hip replacement at the Veterans Administration hospital in Denver.
- February 9, 2004: He contracted an infection at the site possibly due to his body's reaction to a foreign body.

- November 18, 2004: Don went into see the doctor. Another setback occurred called a lucent zone [16]which was between his femoral stem and bone.

- August 1, 2005: Doctors x-rayed Don's hip because they thought the prosthesis was becoming loose too early.

- August 15, 2005: Medical staff again noticed the "L hip and pins" were possibly becoming more loosen.

- August 18, 2005: Don's pain increased pain with no relief. Again doctors x-rayed the hip and an evaluation was to follow. Don had been taking painkiller Percocet one Tablet. The medication did not help.

- September 12, 2005: By this time Don had been in pain for about six months. Pain increased on every occasion when he put weight on that hip. He could not sleep. By then he walked with help but could not stand for long periods of time so he had to quit work. Don saw the radiologist at the Denver VA. They prescribed Ibuprophen and sent him on his way. He was still in pain.

- September 29, 2005: The Ibrupophen did not help. Don was miserable. He could not sleep and suffered constant pain.

- October 6, 2005: Don still complained of pain in his hip. Yet again as on September 29, doctors took no action.

- November 28, 2005: Don had another X-ray of the hip. Still the right hip did not show any specific abnormalities. Yet, pain continued.

- November 29, 2005: Doctors admitted Don to the Denver VA and ordered a MRI.[17] His left groin pain was not better but had gotten worse after he tried to ride a lawn mower. Pain continued.

- December 1, 2005: Again doctors could not agree with a diagnosis upon consultation. Each doctor thought something different. Yet, the MRI done November 30 showed a change. Don's pain continued with no relief in sight.

- December 3, 2005: Receiving an answer, doctors decided to aspirate the left hip due to elevated lab results. He now walked with a noticeable limp. Also he tried to work but he could not.

- December 5, 2005: They aspirated the left hip and obtained fifteen centimeters (cc) of reddish fluid which they sent for culture.

- December 9, 2005: The culture revealed Bursitis.[18] Don went home.

- January 9, 2006: Another culture done to see if infection grew in the hip was negative.

- February 13, 2006: Doctors performed another X-ray of his left hip. It showed no change.

- March 2, 2006: Don continued to complain of pain in his left hip.

- April 4, 2006: Doctors orders a rheumatology[19] consult because of abnormal results.
- May 11, 2006: By this date Don could not flex his left knee or hip. In fact, he could not sit on his left buttock and extend his knee or hip. He barely lifted his left leg when getting off the examination table. Elevated lab results showed there was an infection or some swelling. He needed another needle aspiration to determine if infection was present.
- May 22, 2006: A CAT[20] scan showed a large amount of fluid around the prosthetic piece. Don had an increased blood count. This meant an infection was most likely present.
- May 24, 2006: Results of the lab work showed the "eosinophilia cells doubled since November 2005." Doctors planned to monitor the situation and put in several consults. In addition, since the scan showed large amounts of fluid collection an abscess may have been present. This concerned doctors.
- May 25, 2006: White blood cells were suspicious.
- May 26, 2006: There was no treatment given for possible infection.
- May 31, 2006: Finally, twenty days after doctors surmised an infection possibly existed they finally performed an aspiration. Don was still in pain and had been since day one.

Doctors did not aspirate enough fluid so no conclusive diagnosis given.

- June 6, 2006: The hospital discharged Don without medication.
- August 10, 2006: Don's left hip dislocated. Don spent six weeks in a dislocation brace.
- August 21, 2006: Doctors examined Don's hip but said they did not find evidence of infection or that the prosthetic was loose.
- September 17, 2006: Don's hip dislocated again. Now it dislocated four times— twice in the brace.
- October 5, 2006: Finally doctors performed surgery and found the prosthesis was "unstable." It needed revision.
- November 2, 2006 to January 13, 2007: The hip would fell out of joint three times.
- January 13, 2007: The prosthetic dislocated and fractured.
- January 17, 2007: Doctors discovered the muscles had torn away from each other. They repaired the muscle. The femur was like a skeleton. His muscle was dying.
- January 18, 21 and 23, 2007: The hip dislocated.
- January 26, 2007: Surgeons operated. Doctors found the muscle dying. Antibiotics were given.
- January 31, 2007: Don's fever said infection.

- February 4, 2007: Another surgery revised the previous one. Don's wound developed staph[21]
- February 20, 2007: Doctors discharged Don with oral antibiotics.
- February 25, 2007: They aspirated[22] his wound.
- February 26, 2007: Surgeons found sepsis[23] while performing another operation. A large amount of the muscle died. In addition an abscess held about 700 to 800 centimeters (cc)[24] of fluid that went clear through to his implant. They drained it and removed large amounts of tissue. Yet, massive amounts remained. Doctors noted muscle deterioration. His wound needed more debridement.[25]
- March 1, 2007: Don went to Salt Lake VA for further implant removal.
- March 5, 2007: Don went through another operation for infectious implant removal. Staff noted a large collection of fluid — about nine hundred centimeters— which enclosed the entire wound. He suffered massive bone and muscle loss. Doctors then implanted a spacer[26] impregnated with an antibiotic.
- March 11, 2007: Salt Lake transferred Don back to the Cheyenne VA.
- March 13, 2007: Don went back to the Salt Lake VA for more debridement.

- March 15, 2007: Doctors removed all remaining hardware along with part of the bone.
- April 5, 2007: Infection and antibiotics increased.
- April 12, 2007: His hip dislocated again. Don finally went home. Ramps or other equipment needed to care for him were missing.
- April 19, 2007: Another infection possibly set in given the circumstances. Don could no longer walk or stand. He used crutches and a wheelchair.

Don had a right to be angry. He went through so much from 1993 to 2007 yet the horizon held more disappointment. We seem to persevere when God is at the center of our lives. God never promised us that when we became Christians our lives would be without conflicts. Our rewards are not on earth but in Heaven.[27] Don certainly knew this.

Chapter Seven
Divided we fall

*... and every city or house divided against itself shall
not stand; Matthew 12:25 (KJV)*

Don went through three years of pain only to find
darker days were coming. His life as he knew it
changed drastically. All beloved outdoor activities all but
vanished because his left hip no longer worked. June 2007,
the Cheyenne VA released Don home. Home health
nurses traveled out to their home because Judy's health
prevented her from caring for him. Like a script from a
movie, his life changed again. To this point he survived
colon cancer, fifteen hip surgeries and lengthy hospital
stays. Yet, he continued trusting God. Don was down
but never out.

When we go through trials, we either run to God or
pull away. God is patient and waits for us to decide what
we are going to do. I think Don ran to God. He continued
praising God for his life. Don always smiled though his
life was in shambles.

God refines us by fire. The Bible says perseverance
brings hope and hope does not disappoint. [28] Don had an

abundance of hope. He did not know when his situation would turn around though he hoped it would. After everything he went through, I am sure he felt his head was just above water. Don reminded me of Job. Job lost everything he had– his wealth, children, wife and his health.[29] Job steadfastly depended on God to bring him though his troubles. Don depended on God as well.

His marriage of over twenty-five years began crumbling unraveling at the seams. Strain and stress took its toll. Don married twice before and failed twice. Marriage number three looked bleak. Don said his marriage began showing signs of wear while he was a patient in Salt Lake. He also told me "It was not Judy's fault." He continued, "This was a lot for a wife to take." So he still honored his wife during all his medical problems. In addition, he said that before his baptism he repented for many sins because he wanted to be a better husband.

When a marriage ends, it is like a death occurred, but in a different sense. We grieve. Sometimes the offending partner hurts the other so badly it takes years for the hurting person to forgive and move on with life. Often divorce brings out the worst. Suddenly, two people who pledged to honor and obey cannot stand each other. Communication and trust disappear and the love that started the relationship dies.

I have learned there are always two sides to every story. I have also learned through the years that men often see relationships differently than their spouses. Yes, even believers divorce. Whatever, the case a long battle brewed. Dissolution of this marriage was going to be hard since

Judy Number Two disappointed Don. It was very hard for him because he hurt deeply. His hurt never left him.

Later while going through his papers I found this note Don wrote to an unknown person.

> *Dec. 16, 2007*
>
> *In Nov. of 2003 I had a left hip replacement at the Denver VA Medical Center. I got a staff infection. In the next couple of years I tried three different jobs, but because of the pain I was unable to work. In August of 2005 the Dr. at the Cheyenne VA Told me not to put weight on my left leg and to use crutches until I could go back to Denver VA to be checked. I was forced to quit my job at the Wal-Mart store. I was in the Denver VA for check-ups twice for 2 week stays for tests. My hip dislocated 6 times and I had to go to the hospital to have it put back in.*
>
> *In Jan. of 2007 the replacement pulled out of the bone. I was sent to Denver VA. In 2 wks. they did 2 hip replacements and sent to Cheyenne VA for rehab. About a week later the Dr. had to take me straight to surgery to take out about a quart of puss & dead tissue. At this time I told the Dr. I did not want to go back to the Denver VA., so I have been going to the VA in Salt Lake City. Since Jan. I have had 6 surgeries, the last in May of 2007, When I went to Salt Lake to have anew hip put in. When they went in, they found more infection and dead tissue so they removed*

it and put in another concrete spacer. I was put on intervenus antibiotics, as well as oral, and sent back to Cheyenne VA to try and clear up the infection. They let me go home in June and I had Home Health Care.

My wife went with a friend to New Mexico for a wedding. She left on a Thursday and was to be back on Monday. She called our Pastor and told him she couldn't handle the situation anymore and was not coming back. A week later my hip dislocated again and I was re-admitted to the VA Hospital.

My wife found out I was back in the hospital and went back to the house. She sold most everything, leaving me my truck and a few other things in a storage locker. I have been in the ECU at the Cheyenne VA since June and do not know what all is in the locker.

She listed the house with a real estate agent and said she would keep up the payments and would let the agent know if she couldn't make a payment. I had to parties that were interested in buying the property for what was owed, but didn't want to pay because the agents fee and are no longer interested

If something be worked out to give me time to have my hip replaced, I would like to try and keep the property or sell it, if I don't get an increase in my VA disability, which is pending. Sorry for the situation. My wife has refused to talk to me *since June and I have no idea where she is at. The reality agent receive a fax that quick deeded the house to me, so I can rent it or sell it or whatever If you will work with me.*

   Thank you for your consideration,
Don Heichel

Chapter Eight
New Beginnings

Now faith is the substance of things hoped for, the evidence of things not seen. Hebrews11:1(KJV)

I've always heard God does everything for a reason and nothing in our lives happens by coincidence.[30] We do not have to see events unfold to know He is working. When we journey by faith, God works the impossible and makes it possible. For example, have you ever done or said something where other people thought you had lost your mind? I have. The first time was when the military remanded my ex-husband to Leavenworth. The second time was when I moved to South Carolina, Colorado, Tennessee, North Carolina, Tennessee, and back to Colorado. I won't go into detail about the other moves. However the last two moves were the important ones.

We lived in Charlotte, North Carolina where locations determined school busing. For instance, living in a bad neighborhood promoted busing to good schools. While we lived in the ghetto Sean went to Myers Park High School (I called the Cadillac of schools) located in the better part of the city. However sometime later we moved to a better neighborhood; then he went to poor performing school. Sean, my youngest son hated school. Though I did not tell him, I hated it too. Hate, I understand, is a strong word. In this instance, no other substitute described our disdain. This prompted change. My son had one year left of high school.

Sean's father, John, Grandma, Evelyn and brothers Kenneth (Kenny) and Brandon lived in and around Mason, Tennessee. For years I drove through Nashville on the way to Mason. I was well aware of Nashville. Nashville is country music, long streets, humid summers, and heavily populated.

I looked up school information, made plans and by May 2006 we were on our way. I used what little bit of retirement I had, to rent an apartment, and a U-Haul trailer which I attached it to our Ford Taurus. We were off and running.

Driving from Charlotte to Nashville was an adventure. We stopped in Cherokee, North Carolina, because I had cousins living there. Without better planning I could not locate them so we found a little hotel and spent the night— Sean, me and Magneto our cat. The next day we were off for another adventure. We finally arrived about two in the afternoon. Upon arrival at our new apartment complex, I signed the last rental papers, got keys and located our two bedroom ground level apartment. Then it was off to purchase household goods. I brought only needed items kitchen and bathroom supplies, clothes, pet stuff and some mementos. After a few months, I bought a condominium.

Sean fell in love with his new school. He played sports—football to be exact. His dad and brothers no longer missed important events like Sean's homecoming football game. It was a memorable moment in our lives as a family. It was well worth the move.

Sean graduated from John Overton High School May 2007. His older brother, Brandon thought it time the younger brother saw more than the south. So they embarked on a journey to the West by way of Oklahoma, Texas, New Mexico, Arizona and finally arriving in San Diego. When my sons said they were going west I was all for it. After all the United States is a big place and deserved exploration, I told them. Now I took my own advice. The South was good however it was time to leave it.

I loved the West. I fell in love with it in 1983 when I lived in Colorado Springs. My son Kenny was born there. The air was clear and the mountains towered above the clouds and people were somewhat friendly. Starting over, being a single woman without children was new. It had been a long time since I considered myself single. As long as I remembered I had had children. Now I had cats.

The West represented freedom and a way of life that inspired creativity, independence and a sense of belonging especially for an African American woman like me. It was a part of the United States that we, as a race, do not often embrace though the southern way of life still portrayed some of the prejudices it has always known. Sometimes we can get so comfortable in our skin change becomes difficult. For instance, I was born and reared in the South.

I reared my children in the same southern traditions I learned as a little girl. For some of us, the South is where we were born and where we may eventually die. I did not want to die there. I missed Colorado and gazing at the Rockies. I missed the West. I lived in the South because that was where my roots lied but my heart was west of the Mississippi. Like my two sons it was also time to start over. It was time to break away.

By October 2007 I rented out my condo to a Sister in Christ named Terri from church. God answered prayers. She needed a place and could not afford her current place. So it worked for both of us. I gave away, sold, and pondered what to take. I narrowed it down to what could fit in and on top my new Ford Fusion.

I began the process a month earlier. I gave a way many personal items to local charitable organizations, shredded papers, and threw away other possessions. In fact, I cut items until an hour before leaving. I finally decided on clothing, some pictures, my trusty computer, bedding, a few files, and kitchen wares. I finished packing my car. Excitement filled the air. I hardly slept.

It is funny the material possessions we place importance in becomes no more than items bought or financed on credit cards. In the end, these items we hold so dear we easily replace in pursuit of better or more treasures. Thus I narrowed everything I owned through the years down to what fit in my little car. The hardest yet remained, deciding what else to fit in my car. I tried fitting more, nothing else fit. It was full. I discovered plenty of room exists in a car except when packing.

I rushed to gather my last possessions. At six o'clock in the morning I ran down my list for the last time Bible, clothes, pictures, movies, litter box, cat food, mementos, bedding, sun shades and money and credit cards. Cats! The car was full. I placed items on top of the car that would not fit inside the car. Magneto sat in his pet carrier in the front seat. I had one pet carrier to pack. My small female cat— Missy, a timid cat, ran to the neighbor's patio. She was determined she was not going. I said she was. I grabbed her. As I held her pudgy little body she fought with all claws. She finally conceded. I stuffed her head first in the carrier. When I was done, I had my Bible (important) clothing, precious mementos, movies (important at the time), pet stuff, bedding, a few pictures and of course two cats now. I was just about ready.

Finally, I was ready to go I left the parking lot the morning of October 31, 2007 about 6:30 a.m. If you have ever traveled in Nashville you know that three interstates get congested very fast. Time was short. We had to leave then. Wasting more time meant traffic. The traffic in Nashville can and is a nightmare if one is not used to it. I remembered it took an hour and one half to drive from my downtown security job to home. I was not going through that again. Experience taught me to be aware because drivers reach exits before they realize. So lane changes are tricky for any drivers. I entered the interstate before 7:00 a.m.

At last, I kissed the country music city goodbye, smiled, prayed for a safe trip. As I drove down Interstate 65 towards Kentucky, Missy and Magneto meowed from their carriers. The CD played gospel music and I talked to God. I asked Him to help and protect me as I was not sure this was His plan for me and my life. Tears fell unmercifully for miles. I trusted God and I knew He was with me. I had faith in Him.

After miles of driving, the Kentucky State line loomed ahead. Yes! The cats quietly slept. The ride went smoothly. Before long, I reached Illinois. The roads were terrible. I prayed for strength and pressed on. I was not hungry. Besides I had a budget to keep and I was not going to blow it on unnecessary food.

I crossed into Missouri. Determined to get out of Saint Louis before rush hour, I motored on. Have you ever been in Saint Louis at rush hour? It is maddening. Cars sit bumper to bumper. I crossed three interstates before finding the right one that read Kansas. Even as carefully as I planned this trip I still ended up in part of the late afternoon rush hour traffic. Motorists were on edge. Of course, construction zones did not help the situation. It was getting late and tiredness crept throughout my body.

Again, determination motivated me to get out of "The Show Me State" and cross into Kansas. The most tedious part of the two day trip lay ahead. Kansas was boring, long and a monster state to drive through. It was evening as I approached the Kansas border. The sun was setting. I was not where I wanted to be however Topeka sufficed. I decided to drive through Topeka after looking at my gas gauge. I did not stop for gas. That was a mistake! My gauge read quarter of a tank. I panicked. Suddenly to the left of Interstate 70 stood a gas station—which was the only one for many miles. The sign read Unleaded, three dollars a gallon. I stopped!

The cats still quietly slept as the little Fusion happily hummed down the dark, lonely interstate. It was time to stop somewhere anywhere. I had driven twelve hours straight. We stopped in Fort Riley, Kansas. The next morning after driving for a while the car needed repairs. Lewis Ford graciously offered roadside assistance and towed my car their dealership. Missy, Magneto and I spent another night in the state of Kansas. By 11:00 a.m. we were on our way again. However, as before Missy decided not to go. Once again, I stuffed her head first into her carrier.

After traveling all day I reached Goodland, Kansas near the Colorado State line. I changed my clock to Mountain Standard Time. Yes! Midnight November 2, I wheeled the car down Nevada Avenue. I could not help noticing the Rocky Mountains' silent command of the night sky. After a little effort I found my apartment. I leaped out of the car walked up the stairs to my second floor apartment as my lungs struggled to adjust to high altitude and cold wind. I found the key and opened the green door. I was home. I unloaded the car, fed the cats, showered and stretched out on the carpeted floor in my little one bedroom place as I listened to leaves stirring outside I settled in to sleep.

Colorado Springs took me back to my first trip to the West. The city had grown a lot however I still recognized some streets and landmarks sadly new buildings stood where some had died.

Two weeks later, I found a job with Cheyenne Mountain Security Company. I worked odd shifts until I got a second job with Guardsmark Security. I needed more money because CMS one only paid minimum wage. So, between the two I worked twelve hour shifts every weekend and eight hour shifts during the week.

The only perk of my second job was free lunch. The five star restaurant at Kissing Camels resort served excellent meals. Needless to say employees ate rather well. Most of the hotel staff like myself, had very tight budgets, or where college students. College students get by the best way they can.

Yes, I was a forty-eight year old college student. I went to college on line and was close to graduating with my Associates degree. However, I wanted the educational silver lining which meant another eighteen months of school. I was determined to have an education. After all, my sister, Annette graduated from college completing her Bachelors in Business and my brother, Jamie graduated with a Bachelor in Communications. I was not going to be the only one without a degree primarily because my mother always thought I was going to be a nursing assistant forever. I wanted to prove her wrong.

Thanksgiving 2007, I had lived in "The Springs" twenty-five days. A new friend, named Terri invited me to dinner. Terri was active duty Air Force stationed in there. Through her I met her father Bob who I developed a relationship. He suggested I apply at the Veterans

Administration Hospital where he lived. I did. I believe the Lord used him to help me with my journey.

I applied and got the job as a nursing assistant. I started moving to Cheyenne, Wyoming. Never in a million years would I have ever thought of living in Cheyenne. Before I moved, I visited Cheyenne on several occasions. The first time was while traveling for duty as a member of the North Carolina Air Guard. Guard members got used to logistics. For instance, North Carolina flew us to our destination then another state, depending on the mission, picked us up. On one occasion The Wyoming Guard flew us home. Imagine that! Still today, I have the utmost respect for the C130 pilots and flight crews of any state. These men, women and aircraft are still and will always remain unsung heroes. The second time, I went to Wyoming was for medical care. I drove three hours to see a doctor. I must say I enjoyed these trips. I had time to think and ponder life. Therefore, I did not have anything to lose by moving once more.

My friend, Bob also helped me load some of my possessions. Again, I gave furniture away. How soon we accumulate things in a short amount of time? I found an apartment and took care of business with my old apartment manager. I was off and running again.

I found it ironic the very place I dismissed as a place to live was where I ended it up. I thought of other places I would have rather lived such as Colorado of course, Alaska, California and Washington State –not Wyoming. After all, I visited the state twice which was not long enough to form an opinion. Here again, God decided where He wanted me to live not me. Just when a person thinks they have all the answers God comes along with a different one.

Chapter Nine
At First we meet

For when we fall, the one will lift up his fellow; but woe to him that is alone when he falleth; for hath not another to help him. Ecclesiastes 4:10

Having divorced several times, I always felt the right man waited for me. At first, I gave God specifics—Christian first, then blond, gray or black hair; green or hazel eyes and tall, slender build. He had to like children and animals because I had three sons, and two cats. Finally, my ethnic background or education could not intimidate him. I wanted someone to lead a Godly household. If you notice, everything I thought about was what I wanted in a mate. God knew who I needed.

As my specifics go, appearance went out the window. As we age our bodies change. For instance, men may develop rounder mid-sections or women lose their girly figures. Media programs influence us by labeling characteristics of prospective mates. They have to be this or that. They cannot be this or that. We forget God made each of us therefore, it does not matter what we look like. What matters is this: we accepted Christ as our savior; the

Holy Spirit lives in our hearts, and we follow the Word of God not what society expects.[31]

I am a firm believer we get so wrapped up in worldly perceptions; we forget about God's idea of a mate. We want this and that instead of looking for spiritual qualities. I am sure, that is where I made mistakes in years past. First, I was not a Christian. Second, I did not allow God to pick my choice. I picked individuals who did not have my or my children's interest at heart. Oh sure, they were handsome and tall, but none of them had money (smile) nor did they know God. Big mistake! So I lived and learned as we all must do.

I went to work at the Veterans Administration. By today's standards it was a good job. I worked every other weekend and had some holidays off and they paid well. I had been a nursing assistant practically all my life. I started while in high school in Health Occupations. However, many years ago, I aspired nursing as an occupation. I wanted to be like the African American nurses who so gallantly took care of the sick at New Hanover Memorial Hospital— the hospital I first worked at as a teenager.

So, I took classes in high school to prepare me for that journey. You know Chemistry, Algebra, two years of French and of course I took the SAT. Successful high standardized test scores meant college. My scores meant no college. So, I went to college part time taking one class at a time proving myself. I did. By the grace of God I excelled in any classes I took. Years later, I was in college still excelling. Though I loved being a nursing assistant I really wanted to be more. So again, my journey took me to an unexpected place or at least for me not for God.

Bob and I continued our relationship. This relationship did not turn out well. However, God uses terrible circumstances for his benefit I believe. Had I not moved to Colorado Springs, I never would have met his daughter Terri. I would not have met Bob who urged me to move to Cheyenne. I will always be grateful for that however other parts of the relationship left my heart in many broken pieces. (I understood Don's struggle to forgive because I struggled to forgive Bob.)

I searched for friends. My friend, Pat lived in North Carolina. Then I met new friends Corina and Matt Sealy though at the time we were not good friends. Since, God mended that relationship. I was lonely.

Cheyenne in the winter is true to its heritage, the west. Winters are cold and long. People go out but stay in if that makes sense. We become a state of people yearning for spring.

As time passed I found Cheyenne to be charming in its own way. I remembered reading about this city of long streets on the internet before I moved. From literature, every piece of information I read said occupants hated it or could not wait to leave. Therefore, one or two opinions exist— either people hate it or love it there is not an in-between.

Cheyenne is large enough for the Weather Channel to place it on a weather map yet small enough that if you stay here long enough everyone knows someone. However, a person can conceivably get lost here and not see people for days, months or even years.

In summer, Cheyenne is alive with Cheyenne Frontier Days[32] showcasing horses, carriages, costumes, rodeo, food, more food, concerts, rodeo royalty and parades for the two week long yearly event. Other than that, it is, some would say a boring place to live. Crime is relatively low, and children go to good schools. Prairie winds blow in the background like a movie back drop. If a person stands at the right altitude in the city, they see nothing but open land and mountains. If you drive down Dell Range Boulevard, the longest street in Wyoming, you will see every retail and eatery from Wal-Mart to Olive Garden. The Veterans Administration campus sits about three minutes (if that) from Dell Range. Its location sprawls land using close to the entire block on one side of the street.

I worked at the long Care Facility or old school word, nursing home. That was where I met Don, Mary, Brenda, Naleca, Rita, Tammie, Dr. Cassidy, and Linda. These people were very important to Don. They were in a word his inner circle.

The nursing home sat away from the main part of the hospital. Very long corridors divided the space into north and south wings where two small nursing stations rested. Each room contained one, two or sometimes three veterans. Some like Don had single rooms with baths. As far as long term facilities goes this was a dream compared to some places I worked. It did not smell like urine. At times it smelled like cleaning chemicals which was better than urine any day.

The first day on any job is learning about facility expectations. We sat through the never ending boring classes—sexual harassment, blood borne pathogens, computer security, confidentiality and computer generated lessons.

Through the grapevine, I heard of nursing assistants falling in love with patients. I quickly made up my mind I was not one of those women. I also said to myself, I was not going there. Besides these guys did not have money. They lived off government pensions.

March 4, 2008 I met Donald Walter Heichel. I heard stories about Don's life. I did not like Don when I first met him. Though by the time I met him, he had been a transitional resident (a person who could go home) at the home for about nine months.

He sat in his big black motorized wheelchair by his room. Don did not have a left hip. He stopped me as I walked past. Don wanted to talk to anyone he thought would listen. I did not have time. He tried telling me about his wife every chance he got— when we passed in the hall, at the nurse's station or while I made his bed.

At any rate, I was still in a relationship of sorts. I needed to concentrate on work and school. He was my patient. So, I half-listened to what he told me while making his bed or helping him ready to shower. For, the most part Don was self-sufficient and did not require much but an ear.

Don's room was about four doors to the southwest of the South nursing station. His possessions cluttered his small room. A single bed sat alongside one wall with a small bedside table. At the end of his bed stood the usual nursing home dresser crammed full. A television sat on top. To the right of that was a very large window. To its right was a built-in closet filled with clothing, games, and art supplies. His one-person bathroom was just on the side of the closet. A small sink and counter with large mirror stood on the other side of the bathroom. It too, was loaded with toiletries, and other personal items. In addition, a plastic storage bin filled with assorted snacks and food stood underneath the counter. No available space remained. Don kept leftover items in two large plastic trunks that sat on the floor in front of the dresser and small chair. His room contained his life.

We often saw each other, as most of the patients did, in the therapy room which was a patient room converted to a workout room filled with modified equipment. It was a peaceful place away from noise and unit business. Several large windows allowed large doses of sunlight to bath the room. The most caring lady named Linda (Don's friend) pampered residents with light exercises catered to their individual needs; ice cream, coffee, milkshakes, laughter, and an ear. She spoiled all who came through her doors so the veterans loved her.

Don always smiled when I passed him in the hall. On sunny days he roved outside or to the nearest Safeway store across the street always returning with several sacks of food. He often went to the Canteen to eat during the day and brought food back to place in the residential refrigerator. Don complained food at the nursing home was terrible so he ate out or brought food in as much as possible.

By the end of April the weather cleared enough for Don to travel outside the facility more. It is a well-known fact it always snows Easter Sunday. After that the weather begins clearing and spring finally comes to our neck of the woods. Ah! Glorious spring! Spring meant shorts. Don loved wearing shorts and tees. His legs began showing signs of spring by a developing tan. His arms below the tees were also beginning to tan as well. He wore his black baseball cap displaying the U.S. Army Veteran logo and moccasins most of the time.

I soon learned there were few persons in the facility who did not know his story. They told me his wife left for a wedding and did not come back. Don was heartbroken at first but with many friends, mostly trusted nurses he began mending.

By May 2008, he had a severe set-back. His hip gave him trouble again. Infection set in. He was bedridden and given massive amounts of antibiotics to combat the infection. His last hope for a hip died. Don was heartbroken again. He wanted a normal life—go fishing, and hunting and to enjoy his remaining years without using crutches or a wheelchair. He stayed in bed for about a week. Don said that he believed in God. He knew God would bring him through disappointment. He never gave up hope.

His strength impressed me. He continued smiling through these circumstances. By this time, though Don had gone through enough to have broken any other person but he remained strong. To date, he had lost his hip, his employment, his wife, his animals, his home, his independence and his relationship with his sons. So in effect, he had lost all that was dear.

Don was mobile again. We talked a little more each time I worked. A friendship started slowly like a spark. It was hard to work there and not become friends with patients. Primarily they saw us more than their families. We were in their lives daily. Most often we were there when their families were not. The facility forbade friendships but that was a hard rule not to break. His story moved me. How could it not? This man had been through so much. So now I added Don to my list of friends.

By the middle of May my relationship with Bob disappeared. We did not socialize more than commuting the hour to Fort Collins for church. I stopped going to Bible talk held at his house. My heart ached. I felt betrayed. Don was a welcomed distraction who unknowingly helped me. Part of my heart was not giving an inch to anyone. Therefore I placed silent stipulations on this friendship. I was not getting hurt again. We could only be friends at work. I decided not to accept phone calls and no other communication. I was adamant about that. I needed my job. Don wanted another friend. He kept his distance and followed house rules. Don was still hurting. I honestly did not think he wanted a relationship other than friendship.

Betrayal leads to different directions. Don withdrew for a while then slowly emerged with reservations whereas it caused me to shy away from romantic situations. I do not think he trusted women farther than he could see them. Even though he thought about me, I do not believe he trusted me either. In the back of his mind, I guessed he thought I would leave him which presented itself later in our relationship. I, on the other hand, felt the same way about him. I was not ready to trust yet. I guess we both were in the same boat. We needed proof of trust. We needed to trust before this relationship progressed beyond friendship.

We also need to trust God's judgment not our own. I took a step backwards. I trusted God to get me to Colorado Springs. I trusted Him to help me move to Wyoming. Yet, in a short time, my trust waned. When I look back, I lost sight of who I trusted.

Chapter Ten
Secretly dating

Fulfill my joy, that ye be likeminded, having the same love, being of one accord, of one mind. Philippians 2:2 (KJV)

June came. Trees filled with leaves and grass turned green. Early summer arrived displaying opulent sun filled skies and warm temperatures. It is funny how stipulations change as hearts melt. My heart melted. It still hurt but not as bad though at times I masked hurt by smiles and polite conversation while dying inside. I hid my feelings at work. Once inside my little Ford, I cried and prayed. It still felt like someone ripped my heart out but it was slowly mending. We learned professional faces as nurses and assistants. It became a part of our professional demeanor.

This evening had been a long one. Everyone had a problem. We were busier than normal. The long evening turned into a longer night. By time we tucked patients into bed most appeared to be sleeping or resting except Don.

I sat at the south nurse's station charting. I do not

remember the date although I clearly remember our short conversation. My body ached. I wanted to be alone with my thoughts and the computer. Mostly, I desired to go home to shower and sleep. Lights dimmed as the evening shift of about eight readied for the oncoming shift.

Don hardly went to bed before midnight. He positioned his chair in perfect alignment with the wheelchair portions of the desk of the nurses' station. He clearly had something on his mind. He dressed in his usual attire of shorts and pocket tee shirt that showed his well-tanned legs and arms. To be honest, I loved looking at his legs. I continued charting information in the computer barely looking up to acknowledge him. I was behind. Oh well, what was two minutes of my time?

Don's black baseball styled hat tilted a little as he look up from behind his wired rimmed glasses.

"I'm so bored." He said with a matter-of- fact no big deal smile.

His statement caught my attention. I looked up from the computer. 'Have you tried dating?' I replied. (I was not talking about me.)

Don told me, he tried calling a woman he met who was the daughter of a resident. She never returned his calls. It did not work out. He thought he was too old. I told him, he was not too old. He smiled a wide grin but then sobered responding back.

"What would anyone want with me? I am old, fat and crippled."

I must admit his answer caught me off guard. My question to him caught him off guard, too. Don told me later, he had to think about my question. At the same token, my answer back to him was,

'It doesn't matter what you look like or what your disabilities are.' From what I had seen, I felt he was sincere and a kind hearted man.[33]

Don reminded me of a trinket someone threw away— unloved and unwanted. Don told me later he thought about my reply. After all, his wife left him because he was old and crippled. She felt she could no longer cope. He smiled and quietly pointed his wheel chair towards his room. I finished charting. My co-workers appeared, not knowing Don and I just had one of the most important conversations of our lives. (The next important conversation came later.) The two minutes, I gave him turned into about three. The conversation lasted a lifetime.

My head spun as I am sure his mind did as well. I thought about that conversation on the way home. It was no longer a mindless drive to my small apartment. My mind whirled with what ifs. Did that conversation just take place? Did it mean what I thought it meant? Was I dreaming? I had so many questions but no answers. One thing I was sure of was that it was not chance and those three minutes was going to change my life. I was sure of it.

The next day was an ordinary day at work. Don and I spoke but did not talk about our conversation from the night before. It was as if we both absorbing the shock of impending love or romance or whatever. I did not think Don had ever considered dating again much less dating a Black woman. I found out later it certainly crossed his mind.

Slowly we began talking more. We began talking short amounts of time then we began talking for hours. I added him to my calling plan. I had two reasons for adding him to my plan— one Don was an independent man. He liked roaming the streets in his chair. Second- —I wanted to talk to him more and really get to know the man called Don. We had the freedom to talk whenever we pleased when I was not at work. I found out many facts about him. We found that we had a lot in common.

First, we both believed in God. We were veterans. A special bond exists between veterans. We are naturally drawn to each other out of respect and service to our country. It does not matter the service or time of service: World War I and II; Korea, Vietnam, Cold War, Desert Storm-Shield, new veterans, National Guard, Reserve, Navy, Army, Marine, Air Force, Department of Defense civilian or dependents. There is something about us that other people do not understand.

Second, we were both in law enforcement. Don was a civilian police officer and Chief and I, a member of Air Force Security Forces. We were passionate about law enforcement and criminal justice. Third, we liked to woodwork, paint, play guitar, and work with our hands.

One evening while sitting at the nurses' station with other members of the team, a criminal justice topic came up. At any rate, I do not recall the question but the answer was felony. Don and I both said it together. Everyone looked at us with I can't believe they just did that look. Don and I smiled.

Budding romances are so much fun especially when it is new and forbidden. We had a secret only known to us and God. One moment I did not like him while the other moment he had completely stolen my heart by his sincerity and Godly love. It shows that just because we plan the way we think our lives should go does not mean it is so.

We remained very low keyed at work though anytime away from the facility was our time. On Sundays after church Don and I met at a local restaurant called Taco John's for lunch. We sat and talked for the longest time. Sometimes we talked about current events while other times we talked about our relationship. It was not unusual for Don to ask me to meet him at a certain place. Don asked me to meet him in the parking lot of East High school after we left Taco John's. East High School was only about a block from the VA. I arrived first. I sat in my little Ford with the door opened toward the school. Don wheeled around to the passenger side of the car. Then he asked me if it was all right if he kissed me. I said yes. It was an afternoon to remember. Excitement and nervousness filled my thoughts. It was the sweetest kiss. That was it. I was his.

July rolled around. I still drove to the Fort Collins Church. I was always in Cheyenne before time for work. Don as customary kept busy when we were not together. There was always a new task to attend like tending to his massive amounts of plants in the greenhouse, feeding squirrels or crows and of course, shopping.

Don loved shopping. He shopped more than anyone I ever met. He shopped more than I did and I loved shopping, emphasis on loved. Most times he brought back food, music or something he felt he could not do without.

Several Sundays later after church, Don suggested shopping though he did not have room in his tiny space to put another item. He rode his wheelchair to Big Lots which was about a mile away from the VA going south. I met him there. We spent hours in Big Lots and our local farm store called Murdock's. Don loved tools and outdoor equipment and dreaming of buying all he lost. Today, he needed to add newer finds in his storage locker.

About three miles separated the VA from the locker. He drove his green GMC truck. That meant he hitched his long trailer onto the back of the truck. He wheeled his chair onto it and tied it down. Then using crutches he walked from the back of the trailer to the truck. Don did not mind. Activity kept his mind off of his impending divorce which was not going well. It also kept his mind off the other events in his life. Though every time he saw his possessions stored somewhat haphazardly placed in the locker he became saddened by what he lost.

During most visits to the locker, we worked. Up until now, organizing and moving contents tired Don out because he tried doing these tasks without help. He had help now. We opened the very heavy white rolling door and peered in. There was stuff from the door the back of the storage unit. Don tried weaving and bobbing his way through the mess to no avail. He gave up. Renting and moving everything to a bigger unit was the plan. Today we sorted and moved some items. For now that was enough. He suggested lunch.

Our favorite eating place became Village Inn next to La Quinta; the one Don and Judy managed alongside Interstate 25 North. Two Village Inns served clients in Cheyenne—one about a block from Daylight Donuts shop and the other by The Home Depot. We loved the one by The Home Depot because of it's out of the way location. We ate there quite frequently whenever we visited his storage unit. Each of our visits yielded a large meal and dessert. We took as long as we liked when we visited the restaurant. We needed relaxation and conversation away from the VA. When he relaxed, the smile came as easily as a rising sun. Most times we dreamed of our future and made plans.

Beginning August the weather begins to show signs of fall. Trees start baring and wind increases. A few good days remain for hanging out freshly washed laundry as I did in my old apartment but for the most part it gets chilly. Bob and I occasionally kept in touch by telephone only when necessary. Even though the relationship had long since ended Bob and I needed to go south so we planned a trip back to Tennessee and Alabama. Bob's daughter Terri deployed and the grandchildren moved to Alabama with her husband who worked for Department of Defense. I on the other hand, wanted to see my granddaughter living in Birmingham and check on my condo in Nashville. We planned for late September.

August 24. Don invited me to his Church. This Church, formally Don and Judy's church hid on an off street. He introduced me as a nursing assistant from the VA. I was the only African American in the congregation. Pastor Jon Laughlin and some of his congregation welcomed me with smiles and approval. I had admit, I was a bit nervous. I went to United Methodist Church because Don wanted me there. I also felt couples should share the same church. Consequently, this church held many memories for Don some of them bad. Yet he continued going. I never understood why. Most of the congregation knew Judy and knew what had happened.

Before I left for Nashville September 20, 2008 we talked about the trip. I assured him there was nothing between me and Bob though he knew of him and about our relationship Don, to his credit, was the most understanding man I had met. He never grilled me about this relationship. I loved him for that. Several days before I left I was assigned his end of the hall and went in to make his bed. To this day I cannot remember when we talked marriage. I know I said,' we should get married.' Don remained silent for a minute. Then he replied, "We need to wait so we would have been dating for at least nine months. I said, "Okay." That was the end of the conversation. It wasn't the best proposal. It was obvious he had been thinking about it too. He told me to pick out a ring and to get what I wanted because I was the one wearing it. I picked a very small diamond. It was more like a promise ring. I was proud of this ring and its implications.

I waited nine years after my last marriage before dating. My relationship with Bob hurt. Don was different. I am sure his ex-wives beg to differ. He was kind, gentle, understanding, a good listener, strong in the Lord, and unselfish. Most of all he loved me. No matter what we did, we did together. It was the kind of relationship I had always dreamed of but never had until now. So at forty-eight, I found my soul mate, the love of my life. I was not letting go for nothing in this world. He was not perfect, no one is. Faults surfaced. He still hurt from the break-up with Judy. He talked it about often. Talking was healing. I understood that but it did not make it easy. Healing took time.

God worked this out. I left a terrible heart breaking relationship for one of peace. I prayed for God's protection before leaving Cheyenne. It was certainly a grin and bear it ride. Bob had no idea I was still hurting. I can say, this was one ride I really hated but economically it made sense. I missed Don so much. I called him every opportunity I got especially when I checked into a flea bag motel in Birmingham. I did not sleep. Don and I talked all night. I was afraid to go to sleep. After four days, I drove home-home to Don.

By the second week of October the charge nurse called me into her office to discuss my relationship with Don. Suspicion started the night that I worked my usual three to eleven shift. Upon leaving I decided to stop by Don's room. I kept on my coat as my intention was to go home and rest. It had been a long day and I still homework to finish. At any rate, I stood across the bedside table. Don sat on his bed. I left his door cracked so anyone walking or standing at the door heard our conversation. Walker Texas Ranger was coming on. Don stayed up to watch it. He loved Chuck Norris. Don said on several occasions Chuck Norris was his hero. Time passed 11:30 p.m. was now 12:30 a.m. which suddenly turned into one o'clock in the morning. We were still talking. Finally, I slipped out the door at about 1:30 a.m.

The next day was not good. The charge nurse told me they fire nursing assistants, or take them to court because of inappropriate behavior. It was my job or Don. The third time to the office resulted in a written reprimand (though they did not called it that). After that I hated work. Several times I went into Don's room and cried because of it. This hurt him deeply. He did not like to see me cry. I began looking for another job. The choice was clear. It was Don not the job. I could always get another one. After all I had my Associates Degree. I was intelligent and most important I had God on my side.

Nurses decided to change the work schedule so I had to work the other end of the center. Don always rode down to see me only staying for a minute. We passed each other in the hall and tried not to smile but we did. Don finally told a trusted friend. Our friend was very excited to say the least. So, four of us knew– our friend in Cheyenne, Pat, Don and me.

November was cold, snowy and gray. Don and I went to the Fraternal Order of the Eagle's Club for Thanksgiving. It was our first official Thanksgiving as a couple. We met his friend Opal. The end of November, we went to court. The judge continued Don's divorce proceedings again.

By now, I had one final interview with Laramie County School District Number One for the paraprofessional position which is a politically correct name for teacher's assistant. I prayed before the interview and went in. It was grueling because about six individuals sat in the interview. God was gracious. I got the job. I received the call the afternoon of my Friday shift during the first part of my shift. The same day I wrote out my resignation as I walked down the hall. It said, 'this is my two weeks' notice. I quit effective November 30. I was done. December 3, 2008. I began working for the District as we lovingly call it.

I was free to see Don as much as I wished without complications. Now I was considered his significant other. Everyone was happy for us. The news certainly took staff and some residents by surprise. We went to court in December. Divorce granted. Don was not happy with some parts of decree or his attorney because it took one year and about two months to become final. It was over. Now, I could plan our wedding. I had five months to plan it. My ring changed from a little diamond to a quarter carat marquis which I proudly showed everyone. Don and I smiled a lot.

Chapter Eleven
One More thing

Give hear to my words, O Lord, consider my meditation Psalm 5:1 (KJV)

October through January 2009 was cold and busy. We celebrated Christmas and continued learning about each other. Our love grew more as each day passed. We were inseparable, where people saw one the other soon followed. We dined out, ate in and planned our lives. We prayed.

Prayer is a powerful tool[34] because we may speak directly to our Father who hears us. He helps us through good times and bad times. He also sends people to help and guide us along the way. For instance, He sent Mrs. Abernathy and Dr. Thomas Cassidy when we needed them most.

While I worked as a nursing assistant from March to December I met the most humble, gracious and sweet lady named Mrs. Abernathy whose husband had been a Colonel in the United States Air Force during World War II. For years he lived at the home now at the end of his life he lived next to Don.

She taught me indirectly to give not as a nursing

assistant but as a wife of a man living in a long term facility. Of course, I never loved anyone living in a long term facility therefore all of this was new and a little scary. Mrs. Abernathy came every day unless she was ill. She tended to her husband in the most loving way I had ever seen. She taught me to love Don's circumstances which led to caring for him in a different way. Mrs. Abernathy reminded me of this verse in Titus that said older women should teach younger women to love their husbands, not gossip, and be holy.[35] Therefore I visited Don every day after work and on weekends. I practically lived there most of the weekend only leaving to go home at night. I did not want to be one of those who left their loved ones and never visited. That said, I will always be grateful Mrs. Abernathy for lessons taught.

Mid-January rolled in. Don began eating Tums after each meal. Any food he ate upset his stomach. He did not like spicy food though he loved Texas Roadhouse Ribs. Those upset his stomach. He complained of feeling bad after eating. In addition to his stomach pains his hip gave him trouble too.

I started wedding preparations. As with any future bride, my agenda filled my schedule—staying with Don, doing homework and shopping. I was now part of millions of brides. I went to my first bridal show at the Holiday Inn here in Cheyenne. It excited me. A young man asked if I was the mother of the bride. I smiled politely and told him No, I was the bride. He gave me the look of: Really? That told me, I was one of the oldest brides-to-be attending this extravaganza. I did not care.

Being an older bride, I had been there and done that of sorts. My previous weddings were Justice of the Peace and ministers only. This was new. I visited every booth, watched the bridal fashion show and brought home a sack full of brochures and ideas. I was like a little girl. Plus my car held an additional stack of bridal magazines. You name it I had it. These were an essential part of wedding preparations. Why, these magazines held an abundance of information and many pictures of dresses. Somewhere, the right dress for the perfect price waited. I focused on the perfect wedding, our wedding. I did not envision a Justice of the Peace, or a quick wedding. I had those in the past. I wanted the fairy tale wedding.

When we were little girls, we played with Barbie dolls. Barbie married Ken. We daydreamed of grand weddings. As we grew older, those wedding dreams still stayed with us. Even now, cable channels broadcasts bridal shows which I watched quite frequently. Besides these shows, the internet is full of websites catering to brides, from gowns to honeymoons. I was now one of these brides who wanted the wedding with all the trimmings (within a meager budget).

My list was simple. Buy the right dress first because it set the tone of the wedding. I combed the internet looking for the right dress pattern. I did not see any dresses I liked. I knew I wanted a shorter informal dress not a formal gown. This was a repeat wedding. Then of course, I wanted a reception, flowers, a matron of honor, best man and music. However, I limited my wedding budget. Don received Social Security benefits and a small veteran's pension and my teaching assistant salary was half of my VA salary. Therefore a two thousand dollar gown or a large wedding was not in the budget.

Meanwhile, Don continued complaining. Nurses alerted Dr. Cassidy. Dr. Thomas Cassidy took over Don's case shortly after he arrived so he knew Don well. His slow, kind smile filled any room he entered. Don's doctor reminded me of a character out of a western drama. He was tall, slender and drove an old beat-up truck. To me, he was an angel because he genuinely cared about his patients. In fact, his reputation preceded him. It was all true. His bedside manner impressed me. He strolled into the small cluttered room and got right to work.

As his significant other, Don gave me permission to stay in the room. Because of Health Information Portability Act, (HIPPA) medical staff did not discuss any patient information without first getting permission from the patient. I was family now.

I had seen many doctors during my many years as a nursing assistant. Dr. Cassidy took time to listen which was an oddity because sometimes doctors do not listen to their patients. Don sat on the side of his bed. He shared his complaints. His stomach ached after meals, and his hip bothered him. Dr. Cassidy assured us he would find out why Don was so miserable.

February 4 the judge signed Don's divorce papers. I picked up a copy. Meanwhile, Dr. Cassidy ordered a MRI and Upper Gastrointestinal Series. [36] I accompanied Don downstairs to radiology. We waited so long it seemed like forever. Both tests were difficult for Don because of his hip. He endured them with a weary smile as always. Though Don's health was an issue, we continued planning our wedding while Don planned our honeymoon. I tried on dresses. Some, I liked but did not buy. My list grew until I made a spreadsheet detailing my ideas. In addition, I kept written copies of lists. I had lists for the lists. Don, of course, gave his opinion here and there because it was our wedding instead of my wedding.

I managed to read a book by Beth Sullivan while going crazy after reading her book, I asked God to come and be a part of our wedding. Her book also helped me focus on some important details that only God and I knew about. Suddenly my free time completely vanished with the addition of doctor visits. Don's health, college and a wedding now dominated my life. The wedding clock ticked down and so did the diagnosis clock.

Mid-February, I picked up flowers and other wedding items from Sara, Samantha's daughter. Sara married that past September or October and no longer needed these items which were a gold mine for me. Four vases of silk flower arrangements made by Brenda, a nurse at the VA, accented my color scheme. I had a starting point. Since we thought about getting married in the Chapel at the VA, I rearranged these flowers in my spare time. The VA Chapel was smaller than the church we attended and would not accommodate large flower arrangements.

We set the date corresponding it with Spring Break and booked the Chapel. Since Spring Break started Easter Sunday, we decided to wed that Sunday. Delbert Hansen, our friend, agreed to officiate. Delbert was busy so three o'clock in the afternoon fit his scheduled. A simple elegant wedding and small reception were easiest. I immediately enlisted the help of my former co-workers, Sam (Samantha) Sara, and Tammie.

Meanwhile, Dr. Cassidy decided Don needed another procedure to further isolate problems. We rode the elevator to One-day Surgery. Nurses treated us well. When Don woke up we talked to one of the nurses. She told us not to worry about our cake. She donated it. God sent her to us. Doctors scheduled another test at the Denver VA. Don hated going down there but we did not have a choice.

March 17: We picked up our marriage license. Yeah!

March 19: Dr. Cassidy ordered a bone scan. We went to radiology for the second time.

March 28: The clock ticked T-minus seven days before our wedding. I placed a wedding invitation on the unit. Don wanted residents and staff to come because he had been there so long and had many friends. I still had not found a dress I liked. My first shopping trip yielded no results. I wanted a formal wedding but not a formal dress. One, a formal dress shouted one wear. Two, spending large amounts of money was not practical. Three, the Chapel was small. I had to go shopping and fast. I went to the local bridal shop at lunch. Dresses were far more than I wanted to pay then to Goodwill and Salvation Army. Neither store had any dresses I desired to wear. Finally, I went to T.J. Max. I left there and went to Dillard's. I found nothing I liked. I went back to T.J. Max. A champagne colored, silky suit called my name. It was a knee length short skirt with matching blouse and jacket. The price was right, fifty dollars plus tax. It was perfect. I found my dress. Then, I needed matching shoes. Plato's Closet had shoes. They hurt my feet but I bought them anyway. I abandoned the white shoes I bought in Nashville for these. Why? They matched my dress.

March 30 the clock said T-minus five days before our wedding. We drove the Ford Fusion to Denver because it saved gas. We found the parking deck, found a parking space and parked. The parking deck at the VA was small. Many people with disabilities used parking spaces limiting parking so taking the manual wheelchair proved efficient. Parking lot elevators were small, too. We parked on the third tier. We rode the elevator to the bottom floor of the hospital, and walked through a long corridor. Then we rode an elevator up to the first floor and checked in. Of four elevators, one worked. This was the case that day. We went to the eighth floor. We finally arrived somewhat on time. Then time stood still.

I took plenty to do. Don checked in again. While they wheeled him back, I found a seat and started making boutonnieres. First, I walked down eight flights of stairs to get to the car. Then I walked up those same eight flights to get back to the waiting room. Finally a nurse ushered me back to where Don was waiting. Before we went home, staff discovered they misplaced Don's shirt. We waited about thirty minutes for an elevator to ride downstairs to address the missing shirt. Finally, it was time to ride the hour and one half ride home not before stopping at Bass Pro Shops. Shopping was therapy. We needed it.

March 31 the calendar counted T-minus four days before our wedding. April approached fast. We chose music. Don requested one song for the wedding. We drove to Cornerstone Christian Supply just off of Dell Range. These ladies helped us by special ordering our wedding music. I added two checks to my list one– for music and two– for packing boxes. We tried not thinking of tests though they were on our minds. We kept busy planning and praying. Don's symptoms worsened. His shoulder hurt and indigestion increased after each meal. He still managed to go shopping for slacks for the wedding. We drove to Corral West in the mall, a store he and Judy worked at years ago. We found a bolo embossed with an eagle in flight and slacks to match his western jacket a foreshadowing event which you will see later.

April 1 was Fool's Day. We had four days to go before our wedding. I was set. I only had one other task to accomplish. My rings were back from the jeweler which had been sized and polished. Our wedding clothes hung in protective bags. I had everything for the reception except for last minute items. Wedding programs needed printing. We were just about ready.

Meantime, we tried concentrating on life together and being a couple. Preoccupation with wedding preparations helped keep our minds off test results. Our wedding took precedence at the moment therefore I continued counting down as brides do. We talked about our honeymoon. I called several hotels. We knew April held unpredictable weather. In fact, people told me every Easter brought snow. We prepared. Don ordered his medications to take with him. It was an easy day.

Dr. Cassidy knocked on Don's large door and entered Don's room. He asked to speak to us about Don's test results. Of course, we said yes. I do not remember what he said exactly. Sometimes when doctors tell patients news it hangs in the air. It did. We heard parts. He quietly told us Don had cancer of the pancreas. It was conclusive. Somehow we both heard that. I felt shock. It was four days until our wedding. I remembered sitting on Don's bed. He sat thoughtfully in his black motorized chair. When Dr. Cassidy left, Don looked at me with the most loving eyes.

He said, " I do not want you to have to take care of me. You can back out of the wedding if you want."

My response was, "No, I am not backing out. Don, I love you. Love does not back away just because of cancer." We both cried.

April 3. Two days before we married the blizzard started. From weather reports it promised to be a bad one. Snow fell heavily with strong wind gusts. Cheyenne shut down. I went to the VA as usual.

Don asked me again, "Do you want to back out?"

He said, "I know it is gonna to be hard. I do not want you taking care of me. He continued, "Judy left me. I do not want to go through that again."

I could not blame him. He still hurt. I said, 'I am not backing out. I love you.' He had heard that before, too. He trusted me. I was not going to let him down. Don had

had too much heartbreak in his life. Someone needed to love him. Again we both cried. Later that day Dr. Cassidy pulled me into his office for a chat. He said he was glad we were marrying because Don could not manage on his own. I thanked him. This conversation made my day.

April 4 a blizzard hit Cheyenne. No one went anywhere. Some roads, streets and businesses closed. People stayed home or dug out of their driveways. Our wedding programs remained at the printer. I tried to get there, but could not. A short fifteen minute trip took forty-five minutes. Fed-Ex closed? I panicked. Life kicked. Now life took all my strength. My husband had cancer and there was nothing we could do about it. Of course, we had not heard options yet because doctors postponed his appointment until after our honeymoon. So my fairy tale had a few hiccups. We would overcome this together.

Do you believe God prepares us for future duties? I do. Since age ten or eleven, I have been caring for those placed in my care, first I babysat my younger sister Heidi, who passed away then I babysat during junior high school and I nursed the ill at New Hanover Memorial during my senior year of high school. Years later, God took me to Cushing Memorial Hospital in Leavenworth, Kansas. More than thirty years I cared for people one way or the other. It reminded of this verse:

> "Blessed *be* the God and Father of our Lord Jesus Christ, the Father of mercies and God of all comfort, who comforts us in all our tribulation, that we may be able to comfort

those who are in any trouble, with the comfort with which we ourselves are comforted by God. "2 Corinthians 1: 2-4 (KJV)

God comforts us when trouble comes. In turn we show others the same comfort he showed to us. His compassion, caring and love is beyond any measure I could ever achieve. He is our role model for extending compassion and caring to others in need. So, I thought about this verse. He gives us gifts that enable us to be there for others.

Finally, it was zero days until our wedding. The snow melted. One would have thought this was my first wedding. It was. I was marrying the man I loved with all of my heart. This was the one I had waited for. I was his and he was mine. I prayed:

'Lord, please be a part of our wedding and bless us. Be with us.'

I did not sleep well because of excitement and anticipation. The cancer was here. It was not going anywhere. I wanted to concentrate on our day. Everything else would take care of itself.

Chapter Twelve
Fairy Tale then pain follows

Your presence is requested at the wedding of
Dorothy Knox Burrell
and
Donald Walter Heichel
Sunday, the fifth of April
Two thousand and nine
At three o clock in the afternoon
At
The Veteran's Administration Chapel
Building One
2360 Pershing Blvd
Cheyenne, Wyoming

Sunday, April 5.

- 10:00 a.m.: I drove to FedEx to pick up wedding programs.
- 10:30 a.m. I left Fed Ex and headed for Wal-Mart to shop for last minute food supplies then to the VA.
- 12:00 p.m.: I arrived at our apartment.
- 12:30 p.m.: I finally applied make-up, nail polish, and styled my hair.
- 1:00 .p.m.: I arrived at the VA again this time to finish final preparations for the reception.
- 2:00 p.m.: We rehearsed the wedding ceremony.
- 2:30 p.m.: We finished decorating the community dining hall. The cake arrived. Don got dressed with help because he was so nervous he had trouble with his shoes.
- 2:45 p.m.: I dressed.
- 3:05 p.m.: I entered the VA chapel. The wedding march started playing. Don sat in his wheelchair with the best man standing behind him. Chaplain Delbert stood in the front of the Chapel. The VA Chapel was small but filled to capacity with nurses, other staff, patients, and friends. As I entered the Chapel Don's eyes filled with pride and love as he turned to watch me walk down the short aisle. Finally after all the customary speech it was time for vows. Don stood with my help. He was determined not to sit. We looked into

each other's eyes and choked back tears as we repeated our vows. We asked Delbert to read this verse:

Charity suffered long, and is kind; charity envied not; charity vaunted not itself, is not puffed up, Doth not behave itself unseemly, seecatch not her own, is not easily provoked, thinketh no evil; Rejoiceth not in iniquity, but rejoiceth in the truth; Beareth all things, believeth all things, hopeth all things, endureth all things. Charity never faileth: but whether there be prophecies, they shall fail; whether there be tongues, they shall cease; whether there be knowledge, it shall vanish away.

In other words Love suffers long, and is kind, love does not envy; love does not boast; it is not puffed up. Does not behave unseemly, seeks self, is not easily provoked, thinks no evil; does not rejoice in wickness, but rejoices in the truth; It bears all things, believes all things, hopes all things, endures all things. Love never fails, but where there are prophecies, they will fail, whether there are tongues, they will cease, whether there is knowledge, it shall vanish away. 1Corinthians 13: 4-14 (KJV)

- 3:30 p.m.: We were married. We left the Chapel and moved down the hall towards the dining hall. Many friends were there to wish us well.

- 6:00 p.m.: We shoved wedding supplies and gifts into Don's room. The pharmacy did not have his medications ready. We left without them though I urged Don to go back to get them. Not having pain medication hurt us later. We changed, finished packing and drove to the Hampton Inn for a night of relaxation.

- 6:30 p.m.: We checked into our spacious room. A king size bed dominated the room alongside a large two person Jacuzzi. My fairy tale began. We hurriedly placed our bags in our room and were off to the Outback Steak House for an evening meal. It was our first meal as Mr. and Mrs. Donald Walter Heichel. It was also our first night together as a married couple.

April 6 we rode the elevator downstairs for breakfast. Don ate eggs, bacon, pancakes, drank juice and coffee. I ate bacon and eggs, toast. We checked out about eight o'clock and were on our way to Deadwood, South Dakota. The drive was long, but beautiful. Many acres of farmland painted the Wyoming landscape between Cheyenne and South Dakota. Hills and mountainous terrain dotted miles of land just below the border as far as the eye could see. Snow blanketed the Black Hills. In fact, snow was so high it all but buried road signs. Smoke bellowed from log homes and cabins just about an hour outside the little famous town. I had never seen such beautiful natural landscape. It was the kind one sees on calendars that make you wish you were there. Don kept saying take pictures but of course I didn't.

- 4:00 p.m. We arrived. The town was small but loaded with all kinds of large, small, grand and ugly looking casinos. Patrons gambled from sunup, to sundown. We rode through narrow, winding streets until we found a hotel. The sign read: Super Eight Free breakfast, twenty-four hour casinos, hot tub, clean rooms, and indoor pool. That was for us. I paid and asked for handicapped accommodations. The motel did not have any. Stairs led to our room on the bottom floor. The clerk said, it was all they could do. We accepted it. Don accepted it. He struggled navigating the stairs though he never said a word.

- April 7: Don felt sick. We ordered food in and watched television. I worked on homework. He apologized for feeling sick. I told him, he never had to apologize to me. It was okay.

- April 8: He felt well enough to drive to see Crazy Horse and Mount Rushmore. The sun shone brightly in the Dakota sky and animals played along the highway. We really enjoyed ourselves. We shopped of course, and returned to the hotel that evening.

- April 9: Don's pain level was at least ten. He

cried. We got in the hot tub. He got into the pool and swam about two laps. I begged him to go the local hospital. He did not go. Pain continued at intervals for the next three days.

- April 10: We rode through Deadwood that morning. We ate out for dinner. Then we went back to the room.
- April 11: We started home. We stopped in Douglas, Wyoming and ate at Perkins. We spent the night at the Best Western there. Don's pain started again. He cried and sat up most of the night.
- April 12: We arrived home mid-morning. Don got pain medication. He suffered a week without it. Finally, no pain ravaged through his body.

Our wedding

Chapter Thirteen
Coping

Wives, submit yourselves unto your own husbands, as unto the Lord. Ephesians 5:22 (KJV)

Doctors scheduled Don's first appointment at the Denver VA cancer center. From what his oncologist said, we were in for a long battle. We did not have options like the Whipple procedure[37] because of Don's age and location of the mass. The Whipple procedure is an extensive surgery involving most of the digestive system. Since this cancer had a low survival rate whatever life Don had to live; we had to do it quickly with as much gusto as we could stand. So we worked hard but play harder. We loved with every ounce of our being plus some. The skies were the limits. We also had to live a life that included God for without Him we were not going to make it

Several exciting events happened in June 2009. First we picked up Penny, a beagle pup, from the pet store then two months later we got Piper, another Beagle pup. We now had two cats and two dogs— four kids (as Don called them). Second, the VA awarded Don a sizable amount of money because of past hip complications.

Don went shopping not small shopping but mega shopping. Don wanted two things, actually more than that. He wanted to replace everything he lost during his separation and divorce. Therefore his list extended several pages. Since the money was not mine per se I did not protest. My role reminded me of Ephesians 5:22. Paul said: Wives submit to your husbands as to the Lord. Don's happiness mattered. He shopped and shopped some more.

Three big ticket items topped his lists– a toy hauler, new truck and house. His first big ticket purchase was the truck to pull the toy hauler which made sense to him. Why buy a toy hauler if there is nothing to pull it? After careful consideration and shopping, Don found the perfect truck. Next he shopped for his dream– a toy hauler. These monster fifth wheels offer ample living space for up to eight persons. Of course it hauls "big boy toys" in the back. I'll tell you more about that later. He bought the toy hauler with some input from me. He continued shopping. He shopped on television, on the internet and in stores. Now we wanted to travel.

Early July we traveled back to Mansfield. It was time I met his family. We had a place to stay, the vehicle and money to go. Don arranged his chemotherapy appointment so he received his treatment when we returned. I packed our traveling house with everything we thought we needed for a two week trip. I loaded it with food, kitchen supplies, movies, clothing, computers, pet toys and supplies, linens, toiletries and the like. Of course, we took his wheelchair and some sporting goods. With all items packed and ready, we locked the apartment, and rolled out. Our first stop was Cabelas Sporting Goods store and campground in Nebraska. We were new at this type of camping so ironing out some bugs was important. For instance, we figured out how to position the fifth wheel so we could hook up water and electricity. Then of course, once settled for the night, we shopped. We decided it was not bad for our maiden voyage.

With the first part of Nebraska behind us, we continued to Omaha. Don drove these miles many times while driving for Greyhound so this was like old times for him. This was like cake. Traveling on, we reached Iowa. We stopped at the rest stop. I needed to work on homework. Rest stops in Iowa had WI-FI which meant I could work on homework on the go without missing school. Don rested while I worked. We were on to Illinois, the headache state. Don expertly wheeled this big rig through traffic until we reached a suburb outside Chicago. We found, what else, Wal-Mart. We stopped midday, shopped and rested. It was easy getting this big rig into the parking lot. It was hard getting it out. The brake pin loosened as Don tried making a wide turn around a small curb. The fifth wheel responded with a dead stop. I heard anger in his voice as it happened. In fact, it was one of the few times I had seen him mad. What a lesson learned! Motorists did not move to help us. We had to figure it out by ourselves. I got out and onto a stored step stool. Climbing in the truck bed I found the pin and pushed in its slot. We learned teamwork quickly. We had to or fail. The crisis resolved.

We drove until we reached Indiana then on to Ohio. Don drove the entire trip with few complaints. Three o'clock, Eastern Daylight Time we finally pulled into Dave and Pat Heichel's driveway. Later Pat hosted a family dinner. I met the Heichel clan, Joey and Todd Dave and Pat's sons; Melissa, Todd's wife; Maddie and little Grady. I also met Don's son Rob and his wife Jennifer and cousin Melinda. Finally, I enjoyed seeing Jim again and meeting his daughter Alex. We enjoyed lazy days of summer in Mansfield. We shopped at the local grocery store for items that can only be purchased in Ohio. Don liked Ring bologna and Jones chips. Don's friend owned Jones chips so Don bought dozens of bags.

Don showed me where he lived years ago. He showed me the Church, where he and Judy Number One married. We also visited his family's graves. This saddened him. Don drove me to Loudenville, Butler, Perryville and around mid-Ohio. We talked, ate, target practiced and relaxed. We stayed for about a week. When it was time to leave, we hitched the toy hauler to the truck secured it, pulled in the slide outs and we were off again.

This time back, we drove through Gary, Indiana. Gary is famous for The Jackson Five singing group and steel mills. Until now, we traveled toll roads at reasonable prices. Trouble began in Illinois which is about ten minutes outside Gary.

The lady at the toll booth said, "You have five axles that's one hundred twenty dollars".

I dug the money out my wallet and handed it to Don. He fought to control his voice. He was mad and getting madder. (This was the second time I had seen him upset.) I heard it in his voice and saw it on his face. He wanted to know about more tolls and charges. So he asked. She answered his question with a question. Yes, we understood five axles on two vehicles costs. Don and I hated surprises. Still fuming, he gingerly guided the truck so the fifth wheel moved slowly out the lane. We reached Chicago. He was still upset. His voice said all. We changed lanes four times before getting in the right one that said Wisconsin. We finally reached Wisconsin. We turned the interstate onto a dark road. We parked for the night.

The next morning we traveled deeper in Wisconsin. We rode up to a sign that read, Wisconsin Dells. Don had gone to Wisconsin Dells before. He wanted to show them to me. People and cars lined the streets. Streets were narrow. Frankly, I did not know where we were going. We gave up on our navigation system and tried free style with the map. We ended up going through the Dells and not stopping. Our big rig did not fit anyplace. This disappointed Don.

So, we rode on to Minnesota. We saw miles of fields and crops. We also gazed at hilly landscape and flowing rivers. Riding and driving tired us. We found a Kampgrounds of America (KOA) campground. We learned by now to ask if campgrounds accommodated vehicles longer than fifty feet. We also learned to use walkie-talkie communication between truck and scout —me. I scouted the campground and radioed back to Don. They did not have pull-throughs. We did not park.

Pull through slots were very important for drivers of big rigs. They are just that. Campers and vehicles pull in and pull out without backing. So, we drove on. We finally pulled in a rest stop for the night.

South Dakota followed. We drove past Spearfish. He, we, found of all places, Jelly Stone Campground. Yes, now it was time for relaxation. We pulled in, paid, and were directed by park staff to a spot that accommodated our rig. By this time, we had it down. Don pulled in. I hopped out and hooked up water, sewage, and electricity. Don stabilized our home on wheels. Finally, we rolled out three slide-outs. We had all this done within thirty minutes. This was teamwork!

We had three days of bliss with a heated swimming pool, laundry and pet walks. I learned campgrounds attract friendly people with a common bond— camping. Vehicle prices ranged from very expensive motor homes to simple tents. Why stay in a packed campground where everybody sees in everyone's vehicles? It is simple. We liked adventure. After three days we packed it up and headed for home. We enjoyed a whirlwind eight state trip. Wow!

Before Cheyenne Frontier Days my friend Pat came to visit us for two weeks. She told me she fell in love with Don when she first met him. He was warm, genuine and caring. Don showed Pat the town, and a lot more. He wanted her to have a good time. She still talks about that trip today.

August arrived. We felt the tightness of our little apartment. Walls were closing in. It was time to think about a buying house. We needed an agent. Don contacted Misty Woods from Number One Properties. He knew Misty from his previous dealings. Misty was kind, very professional and considerate of our needs. House hunting wears on a marriage like decorating because each person has their own opinion. However, Misty helped us by showing homes we mostly liked.

About mid-September, we drove to Denver for our appointment. I do not recall the exact date. I vividly remember the appointment. It was our usual 10:00 a.m. Up to this point his appointments were the same. From now on appointments were set for every three to six months. They drew blood and talked to us a little. This time, his doctor asked him, if he wanted to continue treatment. Don told her yes. He was not ready for that question. It bothered him. As usual, we left and began driving home. Don wanted to stop for lunch. We did. We numbly drank as much alcohol as we could legally hold but still navigate home. We ate. Don drank three large glasses of some alcohol mixture. I was close to tears and my head spun. We tried to drown out reality, disbelief, and shock. Don asked why his doctor asked him that. I could not answer. I did not have an answer though I only suspicions. I believed Don's lab results told a tale. It was not a happy tale. I also believed his doctor knew then that it was a downhill battle.

We were about thirty minutes from Cheyenne, traveling east on Greeley highway. Don broke down and cried. I stopped the car. He cried for a while. I sat in the car and cried with him. We did not expect it so soon. This was the first time death foreshadowed our lives. Now we tried to live each moment as our last.

October 30 we closed on our little house. It was not quite what Don wanted but it sufficed. Our fenced back yard had room for the dogs and cats. We had plenty of room for parking all our vehicles. The house had a garage, and a large white front porch. Our home was the last big item on Don's list. Like Job, Don's health declined, he lost his wife, home, pets, and household goods. He lost it all. God gave it all back. He now had a wife, home, trucks, fifth wheel, woodworking shop, tools, two dogs, and money. He was a blessed man though he had cancer.

Don liked Thanksgiving but he liked Christmas better. In fact, Don loved everything about Christmas. He loved shopping, trees, decorations, and spending time with friends. We went all out, too. We purchased a live Christmas tree, and decorated the front of the house with lights. He was like a child. He hid presents and bought more. He was determined this Christmas was going special. Little did we know it was his last Christmas. As I look back I am so glad we went all out. I cooked a large dinner and we ate to our hearts content.

January 2010 arrived finally. It is as if the longest week of the year was between Christmas and the New Year. In January Don began slowly slipping downhill. More foods upset his stomach than before. It was hard for me but harder for him. He kept on going. He did not let anything stop him. Don began doing something he loved, woodworking.

In February the VA had its annual showcase where they allowed veteran artists to enter their art show. They accepted all different genres of art. Don built a Wine rack. He took his time but had it finished on time. Working on it meant hours of hard work at the Base woodworking shop. He did not win ribbon as before but, knowing he finished a piece that would last forever gave him great joy.

March was full circle. Don took chemotherapy therapy treatments for just about one year. They began losing their effectiveness. We started losing the war. We knew it. It was hard watching see him slowly slip away. I guess the first time we really realized it, was when his stools changed color. Intimacy slipped from weekly to monthly to completely disappearing. He would not hold my hand, or cuddle. I stayed busy. It helped relieve frustration. I cannot image the pain he felt. Men pride themselves on being able to please their spouse. Yet, he could not. He tried to be brave about it but I saw the hurt in his eyes. I hurt for him. This was true test of love. Love was not about sex. It was about caring for someone so deeply it hurts. We coped. Sometimes we coped by praying. Other times we coped with alcohol. In fact, we stocked the bar. I spent more than sixty dollars during one trip to the liquor store. I repeated these trips several times. Looking back, prayer did not suffice. Why? Did we not trust God as much as we needed to trust Him?

We did not trust God enough. Our lives began revolving around pain and surviving. We forgot God knew us because He created us. We saw alcohol and suffering. We did not see God. I never asked Don how he saw God then. It did not occur to me.

Chapter Fourteen
The Beginning of the End

Look upon my affliction and my pain and forgive all my sins. Psalm 25:18 (KJV)

March 21 Don's pain escalated. Though he usually tolerated pain well we spent the most of this Saturday trying to sooth painful itchy skin. We tried everything we knew from cold baths to cold compresses, and finally over the counter anti-itch medication. He cried intermittently most of the day. The pain was intolerable. He gave up. Enough was enough. We drove to the emergency room about seven o'clock in the evening.

The institutional white painted emergency room at the Cheyenne VA Medical Center, like most hospital emergency departments, possessed a cold, impartial, may I be of service feeling. A receptionist seated behind the window obtained all vital information, name, and social security number. She politely placed an armband around Don's wrist and asked him to update his personal information. We sat and waited but not patiently. A nurse clad in scrubs finally called Don back to a smaller room. She performed the necessary pre-screening: blood pressure, temperature, reviewed his medical record, and asked questions. When finished we sat again waiting for the next step. We sat until called back to a larger room with stretchers and more medical equipment. Don hobbled back defeated. A nurse asked Don to sit on the first stretcher. Each neatly made stretcher sat in straight line along a long wall. Only thin curtains separated them providing some privacy with hardly enough room to move around. Each small unit contained a heart monitor, wall oxygen, crash cart, and an over-the-bed table. Another nurse entered our tiny space. She asked Don to remove his shirt and put on a patient gown. I helped him. The nurse placed an oxygen cannula on under Don's nostrils. She hooked up the heart monitor to his chest and placed pulse ox monitor on his finger (Medical staff used this small fingertip device to check the amount of oxygen flowing into the blood stream.)

Finally, a young looking, on-call doctor, dressed in blue scrubs, sat down at the foot of the bed. This doctor asked Don about his missing hip and the cancer after which he began telling Don his plan to help him. However first, he prescribed medication offering temporary relief then instructed Don to see Dr. Guidry at his earliest opportunity. Don requested Dr. Sandra Guidry take his case before he knew he had cancer. He adored his doctor. She reminded me of an exquisite tall, slender model. Yet, her demeanor exhibited kindness and gentleness and her eyes displayed compassion. The doctor prescribed Ranitidine HCL one fifty milligrams for allergies and itching (This medication is like Benadryl). The nurse gave

Don an injection of Prednisone and a Prednisone twenty-one day Dosepak which is a steroid allowing patients to start with a very large dose then taper down until the end.

I helped Don dress. Don and I were on our way home. We drove in silence. My mind wondered what to say to comfort my husband. There were no words. I felt helpless in the darkness. So, I allowed the motor of the car to purr in my ears.

We arrived home. The fifteen minute journey appeared much longer than usual. Once home, we again settled in for the night. Don undressed and readied for bed. He continued hurting. Massive doses of Prednisone given at the Emergency room did not help. Don sat up in the bed and wept aloud. Through tears we talked about death, faith and his trust in God. We talked about suffering.

He said, "I'm tired of suffering". He wanted to die. We hugged each other and cried together for a long time. How could we not? Don suffered and I could not help him. My heart ached because of his pain. Yet I was numb, too. Don struggled spiritually and physically. He struggled to live and to forgive.

Each person deals with the knowledge of impending death in their own way. Don's fight was to forgive Judy. Though he had loved her for the past twenty-five years he questioned motives. He wanted to know what he did that she treated him so badly. Why did he have to suffer for events of his life?

Don had lived most of his life by sixty-two. As we talked I figured out our lives fall into two categories depending on what we perceive them to be. Don's words reminded me of patients I talked with many years ago when I worked in the hospital. Some of the patients said they lived good lives while others admitted their lives were not good by their or anyone's standards. The latter meant they were ashamed of many acts in their life while the first said they tried to live a life where they helped others or thought they were a good person. We know no one is good according to the Bible. Don echoed what I heard by saying he did a lot of things in his life he was not proud of doing. By Don's admission he was terrible. So there were good lives and not good lives depending on the person's perception of what they thought about themself. Today those acts did not matter anymore. Today he cried and prayed to the Lord, to take him home. Don wanted to die in his sleep. God did not answer yet. He seemed to tell Don he had to wait just a little while longer. Don was ready but God was not ready. Death stayed away.

I also learned years ago the Bible speaks to us. For example, David wrote his thoughts in the Book of Psalm. David talked about pain, sin, struggles, forgiveness, hurt, fear and trust in God. Psalm 40:12-13(KJV) described our situation perfectly. We needed God's help as more struggling days and nights were on the horizon.

March 23 Don went to his scheduled chemotherapy appointment. It was customary for him to see Dr. Guidry after completion of his treatment. Labs drawn that day told why his skin color started turning yellow. His bile ducts were clogging up. Dr. Guidry decided he needed pancreatic stent placement[38] to relieve symptoms. The procedure was scheduled immediately.

Days passed when Don's determination to beat cancer increased. My attitude remained pessimistic though I smiled. He wanted to beat it again. After all, God allowed him beat it twenty years ago and live his life. What can a person say to that? I had nothing to say. We needed a miracle. I believed in miracles. God did plenty of them in the New Testament. Yet, I did not have the faith of a mustard seed now. I saw black and white. I did not see what God could do.

Chapter Fifteen
One More Chance

I had fainted, unless I had believed to see the goodness of the Lord in the land of the living. Psalm 27:13 (KJV)

We steered the Fusion into the hospital parking deck. Don checked into Cheyenne Regional Hospital about one o'clock in the afternoon. We took our time. His procedure was not until about 3:00 p.m. We passed the volunteer table, sat and waited for the admitting office to call us. Finally, after about fifteen minutes we spoke with a lady sitting behind the desk. We made the usual financial arrangements. He signed what seemed like many papers. The clerk snapped an armband around his wrist.

A nurse promptly wheeled him to the endoscopy section of the hospital. Our pastor, Rev. Sandi Dillon and I followed behind trying hard to keep up. After arriving to his small room, we settled in.

A long counter top filled with assorted procedure trays and soft medical supplies lined one side of the room meanwhile large medical equipment neatly placed about the room narrowed walk space. Don's stretcher stood in the middle of the room with the Endoscope[39] at its head. Rev. Sandi prayed for Don and me. I tried concentrating on her prayer but my brain went in many directions at once. She left when the nurse appeared. Don signed permits. Our nurse took vital signs and gave Don's medication through his port in right side of his chest.

The first nurse left the room. Minutes later another nurse appeared. She asked Don to leave on his pants, and take off his shirt. I helped him put on a patient gown. Then another nurse came in. She told us that stenting pancreatic ducts helps bile flow. Bile comes from the liver and aids digestion. Doctors insert stents using an Endoscope. The endoscope, like a telescope with a television attached, helps guide the stent. Doctors insert a small plastic tube in the small intestine and pass it to the bile duct. When finished, doctors remove the scope and sew up the small wound with an incision. This procedure gives patients with pancreatic cancer some temporary relief. Then, they take vital signs again. The doctor talks to the patient and release the patient to go home.

I left the room. While nurses finished final preparations I called relatives informing them of his procedure. I entered the room again and we waited and waited and waited. It seemed like forever. We held on tightly to each other. His eyes and words portrayed the nervousness both of us felt. Some moments we spoke very little then other moments we spoke a lot. Sometimes it appears couples just know without expressing feelings. We knew we needed each other without expressing words. I needed to be strong for him; so I showed a calm demeanor outside, while my entire body reacted to the nervous I experienced on the inside.

Time arrived for me to leave him again. I kissed him gently on his lips. I found my way to the hospital cafeteria, on the bottom floor. These convenient, pricy eateries' main purpose is helping visitors and family members relax by providing food. However, I did not relax.

The procedure lasted a little more than an hour. It was the longest hour of my life. By 4:30 p.m. I entered his room. Don dozed in and out of consciousness. I held his hand. He slowly regained his senses. After some time the doctor spoke with us. The initial stent was not permanent but plastic. If the stent placement held, then within six months, they could place a permanent stent in the duct. I counted six months in my head. That was August. Reality check said he probably would not make it to August. I think he knew it too but hoped for the best. The doctor discharged him from the hospital. Within days, the stents began working. Don's skin cleared up and he felt good. Life was better for now. He felt like himself. We went shopping. As I mentioned before shopping was his favorite activity besides fishing, hunting and woodworking. We played Wii games. We took several trips to the local dog park. Good times did not last long slowly pain increased. There were plenty of painful days where Don purposed to live even if he had to smile through pain.

April 5 our first anniversary arrived. Birds chirped as spring reared its head. This day began somewhat cool, eventually changing to sunny and warm. A Blue cloudless sky lit the heavens while happiness filled our little space.

We celebrated our milestone by tasting the top layer of our wedding cake which tasted freezer burnt and awful. We were no longer considered newlyweds— just an old married couple still very much in love. We made a date for the upcoming weekend with friends.

The first year of any marriage is not without some conflicts and challenges as well as delightful banter and love. Although some marriages crumble in the first year because of trivial issues like finances, infidelity or just incompatibility our issues seemed larger than those. We survived moving, shopping, decorating and a cancer diagnosis.

Cancer and death changes one's perspectives about happy ever after marriages. It certainly changed mine. To date, my experience told me not to look forward to another anniversary with him but live for today. It gave credence to Jesus telling the crowd tomorrow will take care of itself. Still Don was not to the place of no return in his treatments. Therefore another year was certainly possible.

Today I tried putting the cancer behind me as if it never existed. I just wanted to make the most of this day with him. So no matter what he wanted to do I was in. He wanted to stay home as usual he made himself go out. He wanted to shop. We needed to live.

April 27 Don and I went to the VA. Don's pain increased tremendously since the last week. Dr. Guidry called us to her office. She politely said Don was in the last stages. I heard it but I did not hear it. Therefore if we going to travel we had to do it now. We talked about our trip. We began planning.

Pancreatic cancer progresses through four stages [40]. Stage Zero: cancer is there but holding. Cells are present, but not seen. Stage One: the disease is local which means it is in the pancreas. Cells grow slowly. Infected cells are less than two centimeters which equals .787401 inches. Therefore, it is about the size a pen point or a little bit larger. Stage two: cancer spreads outside the pancreas then to lymph nodes around it. Stage three At this point the tumor moves toward nearby major blood vessels or nerves. Stage four: is the last stage of cancer. Cancer spreads to other organs. Don's cancer spread to his liver

A year later, we were full circle from the previous year. When he started chemotherapy, tests showed cancer spots on his liver. Chemotherapy helped rid his liver of cancer.

April 29 I started preparing for the end— Don's end. I drew on past experience. It is funny how our brain reaches into its inner most parts then pulls out old memories. I remembered when my sister, Heidi died. I went with my older sister, Annette to the funeral home. After a while we walked back to room filled with caskets. Annette picked one that suited her. Then, we walked back to the office and talked about money. The funeral cost a lot. God knew I would need that experience in the future. Just think only twenty-four days earlier we celebrated our first wedding anniversary. Now I made memorial service preparations. I also wanted to do this while I could think clearly. If I waited too long I would lose my nerve.

Don once told me he told me he wanted to go to Rocky Mountain National Park near Estes Park, Colorado sit and wait for the end. He wanted to die alone in the place he loved the most—the outdoors. For now these arrangements sufficed.

I left work during lunch drove the ten minute to Schrader Funeral Home. The funeral home looked like a stately two story red brick Victorian. Up close, about ten red tiled stairs, glass doors and a grand entrance separated the business office from the sidewalk. Once inside, eyes easily roamed across the large reception area. The room displayed two Victorian era styled chairs and a large exquisite fireplace with hand-carved mantel. Above a large sparkling chandelier hung from the tall ceiling. Just to the left of the fireplace was the entrance of the Chapel. The one we would later use.

On the left of the main entry way was another larger room were a large wooden beautifully stained black desk too center stage. The desk stressed the largeness of the room but did not over power it. In front of the desk sat two chairs as exquisite as the desk and fireplace. On the right of the desk some feet away were two tall, file cabinets which held scant memories of all customers, past and present, living or dead. Finally along the large picture window was a brown leather sofa and small table. Behind the office was an equally large room adjoining room with another grand fireplace. The receptionist invited me to sit. I began tearfully telling my story.

The funeral home staff members were genuine, loving and caring individuals who walked me through this experience. They recognized my hurt and like so many others through their doors, welcomed me, too. I made initial arrangements putting a little money in a trust.

I learned from working in hospice pancreatic cancer survival rates were slim. About 5 percent of patients die within five years of diagnosis.[41] This cancer had the worst survival rate of all cancers. Knowing these facts made this harder for me.

April ended yet the cold weather still hung around. Winter does not let go very readily when one lives over 6,000 feet above sea level neither does God's goodness and grace. We did not think about Him but He thought about us. Don had one more chance to life now it too, was ending. God allowed me to see Him through others. I wanted Don's end to be a replica of his life. I wanted his homecoming to be happy because he lived his life with gusto.

Chapter Sixteen
The Journey Forward

Yea, though I walk through the valley of the shadow of
death, I will fear no evil: for thou art with me; thy rod
and thy staff comfort me. Psalm 23:4(KJV)

Spring finally arrived in the Rockies. Usually after
Mother's day, snow ends and the real spring begin
followed by the most extraordinary rocky mountain
summer. Yeah! Unfortunately death does not operate
according to seasons. Death did not scare Don though he
was tired. Physical pain at times makes a person tire of the
body God gave them. It makes them yearn for something
better. Don's body pained him but his soul wanted to
continue living

After we moved to our new home, Don continued
on-line shopping. He bought any item he desired. I
remember when we first got the big computer shortly
after we married. Don feared using his credit card on
the World Wide Web. He soon found he loved shopping
on-line. By the end of April 2010, he had purchased all
kinds of hunting equipment and gadgets. He continued
buying more and more items. It was the highlight of some

of his days. Don never thought he would not use any of these purchases. I do not think the thought ever crossed his mind. He knew he was going to beat this. Therefore, he needed the right hunting gear for this year's hunting season. He continued slowly declining. It was doubtful he would see the season.

May 3 we went to his scheduled round of chemotherapy. Nurses gave him the usual medication cocktail consisting of one pre-medication five milligram dose of Prochlorperazine Maleate plus Ondansetron and Dexamethasone Sodium Phosphate injections[42] into his medication port. The first medication prevented nausea which is a side effect of the last medication. The longer name is the actual chemotheraphy drug.

Happy early birthday present to him! Don decided he wanted a canoe for his birthday. He drove to Dick's Sporting store in Loveland, Colorado. He purchased a fourteen foot Mad River gray canoe. I knew if he talked about something long enough, he made up his mind. That was that. Don had talked about this canoe, touched one, and planned. It did not matter the circumstances. This was one more item he recovered.

He drove up in the 1997 green, GMC truck which had seen better days. It was somewhat dirty and smelled of old oil inside. Its body needed small repairs but nothing major. The black lined bed of the truck had a VA installed wheel chair lift. The chair lift helped Don travel independently so he often drove it to the VA.

This green truck rolled smoothly into the driveway. Don displayed the biggest grin I had seen in a while. He got out of the truck and said, "I got it." I climbed into the tailgate and slowly loosened the six straps holding the gray canoe securely to the truck. I lowered it to him. Standing on crutches he gently guided it to the ground. We struggled getting the canoe off the roof of the truck but as before a little team work proved successful. I was amused he bought it. Also I must admit, I was a little upset, too. I could not figure out how he was going to get in and out of the canoe. He figured he could. In fact, his mind's wheels turned. He figured out an angle. Don was good at figuring out how to get around something. When people told him, he could not accomplish something, he did it. He learned that through the years because he had to out of necessity.

May 7 we spent the evening hours celebrating. After all, it is not every day a man turned sixty-three. He saw another birthday. I lived the fairy-tale for just a little while by trying to forget the odds were stacked against him. Sadly, I knew this birthday was going to be his last. In my heart, I felt he knew it too but not want to believe it. We went out to his favorite restaurant called Texas Roadhouse. Everyone who lives in and around Cheyenne knows about the Roadhouse. It is *the* place to eat. I underline the. Not saying the other restaurants are not good but the Roadhouse packs a house. Country music, peanuts, good food and cowboy decor draw crowds. Don ordered steak and ribs, potatoes, an onion and of course drinks. He ate, but he did not eat. His digestive system did not like the food. We gave up and ordered to-go boxes. Eating out tired him as did most of the activities these days. Don took his usual amount of medications and called it a day. It was a very good day. We rejoiced when he had good days because he had so few of those. Itching returned a little time after his birthday. By the week after his birthday he was miserable. He insisted we dine with friends. Of course Don acted like Don by joking and kidding around. They did not see suffering because Don did not want them to see it. He wanted everyone to have a good time not concentrate on him. He pulled it off.

May 11 they drew labs. Don was Neutropenic which meant trouble. His white blood cell count decreased because of the chemo. Neutropenia[43] results when chemotherapy drugs get confused. They cannot tell good cells from cancer cells. So the white cells decrease compromising the immune system.

Since I stilled worked Don drove to his appointment as he had done so many times before. Don dressed in his favorite clothing blue jean painter's pants, red polo shirt, and black baseball style cap. Don drove the gray Sierra GMC diesel. He loved this truck. It was clean, new, and powerful. Don told me later, by time he reached the hospital his pain level was ten. Most times Don smiled through painful episodes but not today. Nurses gave him lots of pain medication while he talked and joked with staff and other patients as he did during these visits. Dr. Guidry ordered blood tests. She knew the story.

We changed our routine. Raw eggs and public outings were off limits. At this point, he did not care about his white cell count. He wanted what he wanted period. So he ate eggs over easy with potatoes. Several routines changed like using a refrigerator thermometer.

May 15 we went shopping. We drove fifteen minutes across town to the busiest street in Wyoming–Del Range Boulevard. Many retail outlets, you name them, sit along Del Range Wal-Mart, Target, Petco, Kmart, and the one and only mall in the city, plus lots of restaurants. We had several stops on the list that day– one of which was Sam's Club. Don liked my netbook. So he decided he wanted one. He chose a red Dell netbook.

Today was soup day. He wanted canned vegetable beef soup. He could not find any. He said, they used to make this soup when he was a little boy. He was not taking no for an answer. However, he could not find it so he gave up. I made soup. He ate very little of it. His appetite waned more.

May 18 Don went to his appointment. Since he was neutropenic before this appointment, his doctor checked his blood count. Later that afternoon, he felt all right so he decided to drive the Polaris for service. Little did we know the weather began turning bad.

About 3:15 p.m., I stopped at the gas station to fill up the car. Standing at the pump I heard, what I thought was the severe weather warning system. No it could not be a tornado? Don left our house for his afternoon appointment. My heart skipped several beats.

About 3:30, a F2 tornado hit Cheyenne. I never saw a tornado up close. God displayed His power. The tornado followed a path in the southern portion of Cheyenne toward Nebraska. Sheets of heavy rain hit the car. Skies turned from light to dark. Finally, I reached him. Don smiled as he always did. He said, "I had to walk to the other building. We did not have power. If it had hit while I was on the road, I would have waited under the bridge". I smiled at him.

March, April and May were certainly turning points in our lives. Life changed. I told Don everything, now I held back. I saw my husband's jovial personality change. Now I saw the private and public persona separate. Don allowed the public see his jolly, good nature because he did not want people feeling sorry for him. What a burden for him to carry! He reminded me of Patrick Swayze, the actor who passed away from pancreatic cancer. When cameras rolled, no one knew the pain he experienced. It was what happened behind the scenes that hurt.

Chapter Seventeen
Home Hospice

Remember how short my time is: wherefore hast thou made all men in vain Remember how short my time is: wherefore hast thou made all men in vain? Psalm 89:47(KJV)

I had heard about home hospice. Today, we lived it as so many other families had. Social workers, nurses, doctors and family members become a team with one focus. We try to prolong their quality of life, grant wishes and help relatives die with dignity. Don was not an exception.

We went into home hospice with two expectations. First, care for Don. Second, make arrangements for him to die at home. Like any journey we started with high hopes and a plan how to proceed. We tried hard to make those expectations come to true. Our plans became our plans. I learned going through this, plans change in ways we do not expect.

Toward the end of May, we began our journey. They assigned Julie, R.N. to our case. Julie was kind, caring, and had the strength of a thousand angels.

Her kind face, sweet nature, caring disposition said volumes about the person wearing the colored scrubs. Julie explained home hospice to us and listened to our few questions. She inspected our house for safety and layout. She gathered information about Don's medications and treatment. Instantly Julie became the face of Hospice.

Days got harder. Don was in so much pain. Julie tried regulating his pain pump to accommodate his pain level. Whenever she got it regulated, his pain increased. His pain level maintained at ten–at the top of the pain scale most days. Julie faithfully rescued us each time.

Days ran together now. We began living in moments of time. Life became moments not plans. From experience I learned as we move through time we plan our lives. We plan marriages, children, homes, and buying all the items we think will make us comfortable or happy. I remember the morning. Don sat in his black wheelchair in the garage. He had everything he owed moved from storage whereby limiting space in the one car garage. (As we age, we store more and more material possessions. Later we find these treasurers we fought so hard to buy are meaningless. We leave them here when we die.) I stood in a tight space facing him and where I could see the sun beaming on the gleaming RV resting alongside the curb in front of the garage. Don had just sat down tired from checking the rig. He checked its generator, batteries, tires and hitch. We firmly discussed the pros and cons of this trip. Don still wanted to go on our last trip. As he gave his view point my mind ran through possible bad scenarios. I had no solutions. For instance it scared me to think of going on the road with him, two cats, two dogs, and a big rig. Supposed his pump stopped? I did not want to go although, I saw Don's side. He wanted to see his brother one more time. Don knew if we went, he would see him. As we continued discussing this situation, Don's pain level spiked. Julie came out and sat with Don in the RV. She kept working with the pump readjusting medication levels while talking with the doctor. His pain ended the discussion. We went into the house. About an hour later, she came back. His pain spiked again. Needless to say, we never went on the trip. It was best to stay in Cheyenne. Besides we needed Hospice support. I believe that is when I realized we were changing. Don moved toward death. I moved away from life with him.

Don worked at forgiveness from the beginning of his illness. Sometimes forgiveness comes easy or it comes hard. Don struggled forgiving the person who once held a special place in his heart, Judy. With that said, the Lord tells us to forgive. He continued working through it. I continued re-packing the RV though I knew we were not going it gave him hope and steadied my hands and mind.

We kept trying to do activities like normal people. Then just what was normal? Our definition constantly reinvented itself. Normal was living each day with vigor and purpose. Then again pain, determination, and an unrelenting spirit to see each day characterized our days. We gardened, visited friends, exercised the dogs, shopped, fished, and tried to live when Don felt good. However, when he felt bad, we stayed in front of the television or talked. We had another day together.

Something else I learned is we constantly re-evaluate what we learned over the years. Then find ways to re-apply what we learned to life. Death is one of those re-evaluations and re-applications. Like parenting, we do not go into phases of death with an instruction manual. No one tells how it will be or how we should go through it. Each of us reacts differently because of this. The end of May, we went to Bob and Linda Thompkins' home for a graduation party. Don looked better than he looked in months. Linda remarked how good he looked. As people say, Don got better to die. Death was coming whether Don or I wanted it to come. It made us stronger as a couple. It made us vulnerable as well.

It is funny how fast a year passed. Life changed quickly. Last June, I was a bride. This June, I was a wife expecting widowhood. Don's health deteriorated faster. He ate little because nothing he ate agreed with his stomach. Pain and medication increased steadily. Sometimes little things bothered him. We were reaching the end of the road.

- June 3 we went to McDonald's. Don loved Chocolate milkshakes. He rarely ate now. So any nutrition was better than none. His body

120

steadily rejected nutrients. He kept losing weight.

- June 4 Don felt good. I had a hair appointment. I was glad he felt good enough to tease me about anything.

- June 8 Don wanted to get his fishing license. That meant driving to F.E. Warren Air Force Base because they were cheaper there. Of course, we checked out three lakes. Don loved fishing. I, on the other hand, did not care for it at all. I went because he wanted to go. He stocked his tackle boxes. We planned our trip.

- June 10 Don was in so much pain. Julie tried so hard to get his pain under control. She called the doctor then with a verbal order, increased settings on his pain pump. However, it did not help. Finally, she told us, we had a better chance if we went to Davis. She led the way. Don obediently dressed with my help. He put on his favorite pants- blue denim overalls and short sleeved pocket tee shirt, flannel shirt (he was always cold even in summer), black shoes, and black baseball cap with the veteran emblem. We were off to Hospice. While we traveled across town, nurses prepared our room. Room ten, it read outside the door. Our room was the first room on the right side of the long carpeted hallway. Don was angry.

Nurses rushed in with medication orders to increase his pain pump. Within minutes pain subsided. This was the beginning of the battle. It was like soldiers marching off to War with no idea when or if they would return. Only, Don's war was pain, discomfort and an unrelenting cancer that was quickly claiming his life. Of all cancers, he had one of the most deadly, unforgiving and lethal one.

- June 11. Don felt good. He wanted to go fishing. What good is a fishing license if it not used? So we planned a fishing trip—one to the base and one to the national park.

Curt Gowdy State Park runs about twenty-four miles west of Cheyenne. Don did not want to fish that day. This was a planning trip. Curt Gowdy is a beautiful State Park. It boasts hiking trails, dirt roads, reservoirs for fishing, and RV campsites. Driving around this massive piece of land easily takes one's mind away from trouble. Instead, they concentrate on the natural beauty of the land. Don loved planning short trips. We drove to this park many times before. Usually, these were planning trips, too. He wanted to see RV sites or check out archery ranges or fishing holes.

The old, green GMC Truck was vehicle of choice because of the wheelchair lift. Don was determined he was going. He wanted to see this park one more time. We did not get there. His pump began beeping and would not stop until we returned to Cheyenne. Don was mad at me because he wanted to go. I was mad at him because I knew we needed to be closer to the center. I tried to understand. Don's character did not allow giving up. He had always been strong-willed. This continued until the end. Knowing this, did not make it any easier for me. This was a difficult afternoon for both of us.

Marriage is a work in progress. It is harder when one partner has a terminal illness. Today was one of those days. How could I do what he wanted? I saw results. Don saw flight. There was not an easy answer. Don wanted what Don wanted. It frayed me. I tried finding a happy middle. No happy middle existed today.

I learned dying and/or medications may distort time, space, or reality. His reality differed from mine. My reality said: heavy medications, disease processes, and death affect your viewpoint. On the other hand, his reality said: I am still me. I want to live. I am okay. Everyone else is not okay.

We had no options but return to the center. About 2:00 p.m. I wheeled him back to our room. He sulked. Nurses hovered around him, made a fuss about the pump, and flushed it. They played with it until it ran. Finally, they decided to replace it.

Don settled down and finally slept. I sat on the small loveseat beside him. Don had his own set of fears mainly I would leave him and never come back. Showering, doing laundry in the community laundry room, and basically living there twenty-three hours a day took its toll. My place was with Don. He needed me and I needed him.

He hated it at Hospice he saw it as another hospital. Having him at home, as he wished, failed. He needed nurses around the clock and immediate support. Time between calls to nurses and medications were too long. We knew this. He became weaker daily. Life moved slower these days. Don slept a lot.

June 17 we tried another day trip. He needed time away. Don wanted to ride. Sometimes riding clears the head by allowing reflection and relaxation. We loved to ride finding new adventures. I especially loved driving through Wyoming. Scenery is breathtaking. We drove to Ames Monument just outside Laramie. We stopped at little town called Buford, population one. Don wanted a slushy. We paid far too much. Prices made him mad. These days, milkshakes were still good but slushies were even better. Today, he tolerated it fine. What a good day! I rejoiced in good days and so did he. It meant he was still living life.

June 18 the sky was blue without any clouds and weather was perfect. It was a little breezy, but for Cheyenne, it was normal. Don picked the vehicle he wanted to drive. We drove the Polaris. Don was still capable of driving. Though, I was not comfortable with him driving. He continued at least for now. Rather than argue, I let it go. Submitting to his will was one of the hardest acts I had ever done. Don's determination and pride usually won.

Pride is one difficult personality trait. It comes in many forms. Pride causes us to argue and it is stubborn.

Pride begins early in life and ends when we die. It holds us back or propels us forward. God does not like pride. [45]He tells us this in the Bible. Don's pride said I am not giving an inch.

Chapter Eighteen
Final Business

*What man is that liveth, and shall not see death? shall
he deliver his soul from the land of the grave? Psalm
89:48 (KJV)*

As we grow from childhood to adulthood, death is far
from our minds. We busy ourselves living, loving and
caring about day-to-day activities. We work and provide
for our families or those around us. As we mature and age,
we realize death is real. We also come to that realization
when a relative or a close friend dies. Yet, after the shock
of their death wears off, in time we forget. By the time we
reach half a century, death comes back again reminding
us it is only a breath away.

Life is short. Death tells us in small ways we do not
escape its grasp. Our hair shows signs of graying and tiny
wrinkles appear as if overnight. We feel new aches and
pains. Medication lists slowly increase. Death is right
around the corner. We will die. The Bible speaks of death
from the beginning to the end. It lets us know we do not
have power over death. The only one who had power over

death was Jesus. He rose from the dead on the third day after his crucifixion. [46]

Don's eyesight dimmed and he lost concentration. I read a book by Mitch Albom to him. Ken Roylance, his wife Helen, and friends from the band, played music for Don and me each Sunday afternoon. Don heard their music the entire time he stayed at the VA. He enjoyed it. Likewise a harpist played for us during the week. Music soothed his soul as it prepared for the journey it would soon take.

Though, Don's eye sight began failing he brought another Bible to read. Our other friends, Jack and Patty Rosenlof came by some Wednesdays to study different passages from the Bible. Don enjoyed listening to us study the Bible. It made his day. He smiled when he heard the Word. Delbert stopped by, at my urging, asked Don if he had forgiven Judy[47]. Don said he had. That news made me happy. As Don changed physically, we helped him spiritually for his journey.

- July 1 his eyes appeared more jaundiced than the day before. He hiccupped repeatedly and slept most of the day.
- July 4 we exited the cottage door to a rather large garden that sat at the back entrances of the three cottages. Different species of flowers and trees populated the area. In addition a large flowing waterfall gleamed as the center piece. Beside the bottom of the water fall sat a very large Moose that bobbed his head in the

wind. A sidewalk, small stream and another pergola completed the garden. We walked the entire length of winding twisting cemented surface. I will never forget paying attention to the bright sun which also illuminated Don's yellowish hued skin. The sun forced my eyes down to his skin. Later we sat outside our cottage. The Cottages were nursing units. Pergolas shaded patios and exits. These patios provided patients, friends and family a place to gather or eat or just reminisce. We used this space many times throughout the course of our stay like we did that evening to watch fireworks.

July 5 Don knew I had to sell the house.

July 6 Don worried about where I would live. I suggested living in the fifth wheel. After all, it was paid for and I would not have had to pay rent. There was room for one. It was sturdy and could withstand the harsh Wyoming winds. Once all slide-outs extended, the vehicle was comfortable. Therefore, I found a campground outside the city that accepted this large monster. Don wanted to make sure it was a good place. He wanted to make sure I was going to be all right without him.

We drove the red Ford. We entered the interstate traveling east. The car purred along at seventy-five miles an hour until we reached twenty-five miles outside Cheyenne. There stood a charming camp ground. The lot rent was reasonable and included gas and water. A maintained swimming pool and grounds finished the site. Don had me ride around it until he had seen enough. He wanted to talk with management. However, the door was closed. I was a bit relieved. Living out this distance meant budgeting more for vehicle fuel extending my budget. It was worth consideration. I chose not to live it the fifth-wheel.

As I searched for a home, God showed me the way. I found a recently remodeled home in my price range. It as if it suddenly appeared out of the air. God is good! I met with Mr. Campbell and explained my circumstances. I signed papers contingent I did not have to move in until September.

The major item on my financial list still remained. I had to find a listing agent for the house and put it on the market. This bothered me because the housing market had not rebounded. I was afraid it would be so it could be months before it sold. Nothing is impossible for God.

July 20 started with a terrible morning. He dressed in a gray pocket tee and shorts. Shorts were comfortable around his swollen belly and he did not have to worry about dressing and re-dressing. By the afternoon, Don wanted ice cream and fries. Dairy Queen was the choice restaurant. We stopped.

We left Dairy Queen and headed to Lions Park. Lions Park is a rather large park situated across four lanes of traffic from the Airport. A large lake for fishing and boating dominated the scenery by its sparkling and inviting water. Its water beaconed even novice boaters in for fun and relaxation. Beside the lake sat several small paved walking trails and bridges. We got out the truck and walked slowly along them. We stopped on a small bridge to eat lunch. It was clear Don had something on his mind. By now his face was drawn and his weight had significantly decreased. Don breathed all of this in as if it was the last time he would see it. Mostly he wanted to talk however he did not want me to answer.

They say before a person dies, they question their choices, or others' choices. Don asked questions today. He was to the point of tears. Supposed the doctors had found this earlier? What if they missed the diagnosis? Why does this have to be me? Why??? What if???? For about ten minutes or so Don tried reconciling the events about to take place. His questioning eyes and worried look told the tale now. He was getting ready to die and he knew it. He still had some fight left. He was still not giving up easily.

He wanted to know if there was another way he could live. It was as if he desperately wanted the person seated in the wheel chair be someone other than him. Nothing I said mattered, or at least the truth did not matter. He was angry. I did not know what to say to appease him. The truth it was God's choice. God knew the way Don's life would go and when he would die, not me.

A paved walking trail around the circumference of the water's edge allowed anyone wanting to walk, jog, ride, or trot around it. We walked around the entire lake in silence- each of us deep into our own thoughts. As I pushed his wheel chair, Don looked at the sights as if saying good bye. At last, we arrived at the recreation center. I pushed Don's chair to a stop where we both gazed at the water and the activity around it. Only silence remained. We left the park as we began in silence. We drove to our temporary home.

July 23 Don waited for two people. Sometimes, the dying waits for someone special to come before they continue their journey. Don wanted to see two people—his son and a friend from long ago. His son, Jim arrived today. Don was glad to see him. They needed time to say good-bye and bond again.

Don insisted we go to Jackson's Sports Bar for dinner. We walked a half block from hospice to the restaurant which sat on the corner of Powerhouse. Don ordered what he thought he would eat. We talked with Jim, and played a game. Don hardly touched the food he loved. He played with the food with his fork. His face and skin showed signs of more jaundice and his movements were slower. We walked back to Hospice. That was the last time the three of us ate together.

July 26 Don called his friend who he met years ago. His friend came by and spent time with us. They had been friends since Don lived in Colorado. Don was happy to see him. They talked for a while. Don's completed his last wish.

July 31 friends continued stopping by to say good-bye. Don was not in a coma, yet, but he slept all day. My friend and Sister in Christ, Pat Walker arrived. I was grateful for her presence and help. She told Don, I was going to be okay. He needed to hear that. He still worried about me but it was nothing he could do about anything.

Don's body began its last stages before death. When a person transitions to death, eye sight goes first, then hearing, and urine output significantly diminishes. They do not eat. As I watched him sleep it occurred to me that he did not care about this world any longer. It held no value to him. All the possessions he fought so hard to save did not matter. It also occurred to me that one day I would be in his place. While we live we care so much about family friends, debts, and just life. As we began our departure, everything we thought was important suddenly vanishes like the wind.

He had one last fight in him. During routine catheter care, Don rose up hit the nursing assistant in the mouth then laid down. This showed Don's unending spirit for life. He went out with a fight.

We had a few more days with Don before he lapsed into a coma. We no longer made promises we knew we could not keep. What was the point? Don gave it his all. He fought the fight. He lived life. He tried to keep up the brave front for me mostly until the end. We lost. He had to continue on his journey and I had to attend final business.

Chapter Nineteen
The End

For when he dieth he shall carry nothing away: his glory shall not descend after him. Psalm 49:17(KJV)

When we die, nothing goes with us. We cannot predict its appearance or time. In an instant, we cease to exist. Our human bodies become cold like ice. Our soul floats away. The only choice we have is to wait for the end. Death does not wait until we decide we are ready. If that the case, we would pick the time we thought to be most convenient or chose to live forever.

August 2 was a significant turning point. Don called for his dad. Don loved his father but he was mad at him too. Don said towards the end Robert gave up. He said his father stopped doing everything he loved. He just sat doing nothing. Don did not understand why. I think that was the reason he tried so hard to keep living. Don wanted to live; not be like his father. I thought it odd he called for the one person who had angered him.

I saw this many times throughout my employment in hospice and oncology. The dying person called for someone who preceded them in death. It was usually someone close to them. Don started transitioning from life to Heaven when he called for his father. I never understood how or why the dying pick certain people. Don could have very well called his brother or mother. He did not.

About two in the afternoon, I placed our home on the market for sale. That was the last large item on my list. It was done. I felt relief and hurt at the same time.

August 3 the telephone rang at 6:00 a.m. Don lasted through the night but barely. Kelly, the nurse on the other end of the line, told me Don was actively dying.

I left home and arrived at hospice within thirty minutes. I walked back to our room which was Don's last place on earth. Several chucks were spread about on the floor. He was bleeding out, which started the night before. Bleeding out is when a patient projectile vomits until the remaining blood excretes from their body through their mouth. Don had so much blood in his stomach. It did not have any place to go but out of his mouth. I could not watch him die like that. It was too painful to watch. He audibly chain stoked too. This is a form of breathing dying persons use when actively dying. Some people call it a death rattle. Patients take short breaths with long pauses in between.

I decided it was best to wait in the Serenity Room. The Serenity Room was a little room just off the family kitchen. It held a large sofa, books and a table. The large stained glass allowed sunlight to bath the room with peace. In the back of my mind, I knew time was running out and so was his power of attorney. I had two last things to do.

Upon finishing errands, I returned to hospice to gather our last items. It was going to be the last time I saw him until Heaven. My lips gently pressed upon his lukewarm forehead. "I love you Don and always will." I would always love him, as he lay motionless in the bed. I knew he did not know how long I was there. He heard me crying, I was sure of it. I told him to go home now. He needed to go. I was going to be okay. I wanted him, to know I loved him more than life. I would be all right. He loved Elvis' songs. They gave him peace. I placed an Elvis CD in the player. Still crying, I walked out the room.

Don stayed alive until God was ready for him. God's time was not Don's time. Don always said he wanted to die in his sleep. This did not happen. God decided he wanted Don to die another way. A little while later, our friend, Delbert, the chaplain, came by and stayed until he died. He also played Elvis's gospel CD for Don as well. Don did not want me there when he died. He told me this several months earlier. In fact, he did not want anyone there. He wanted to take this journey alone. When the chaplain left the room, Don quietly slipped away. It was 2:5 p.m.

I had one more item which was completing the paperwork for my new place. My telephone rang. That telephone call stopped me on a dime. In that instance, time stopped. Somehow I managed to text or call relatives and friends.

Pat and I were two minutes from the street where the new house sat. I walked the three stairs to the wooden front deck. The deck overlooked the next street. In a distance I saw the large, new high school and prairie. The heavy water laded clouds resembled my anguished soul gushing unending stream of tears. It was as if a knife went through my gut. I had never felt anything like it in my life. It was as if my entire insides were coming out. My heart felt heavy and weak. It hurt so bad.

I wanted to go home, not my new home, but our home. I drove like a mad woman. I parked the car and ran up those same white steps Don walked a thousand times. I slumped across our bed and cried for hours on end. My whole world ended. Don went to Heaven. My friend left me. I was alone. I was in pain. I cried and cried yet, the tears kept coming. I was in agony with no relief. I was not hungry. I just wanted to die, too. So many emotions hit me at once. Sadness, hurt, numbness, disbelief, and anguish. I wanted the pain to stop.

The next week God gave me strength to do what had to be done. Keeping busy with chores and memorial service preparations helped. It did not stop the emptiness I felt. Delbert and Lois came by to discuss the service.

August 14 we officially sent Don home at 10 a.m. I said good-bye again. Don's remains filled the beautiful, wooden, custom-made United States Flag Presentation case urn. Tears fell some throughout the service however they flooded during taps.

I had to get through the day. Don was Delbert's friend. Yet, Delbert carried out the service with precision and laughter. My heart ached for him. My sadness was inexpressible. After wards, though Pat was with me, our home felt empty. I felt empty. I did not know where to start picking up the pieces Don no longer said, "Hon can you get that for me or Hon what do you think?" His voice was silenced.

One week after the service: The one joy I had was Don no longer suffered. I dreamt Don was walking around. His face was drawn as it was the last time I saw him. He was happy. He smiled. It was not a forced smile but a peaceful smile. My friend Pat said he wanted to let me know he was all right. A new chapter of my life began.

Two weeks later: The internet was not connected in my new house yet. The for sale sign stood in the yard of our home. I needed to paint the living room, second bedroom and master. All doors and windows were shut. As I stood painting the wall next to the closet, I felt a cold wisp of air on my neck. To this day, I know I felt Don. People say part of grief is when you still feel your loved one nearby. Don was there.

Don 2010

Chapter Twenty
Grief: Not the final Chapter

Blessed are they that mourn for: they shall be comforted
Matthew 5: 4(KJV)

The extent of grief affects depends on the closeness of the individuals before death. When my mother, father and sister passed away I attended their funerals however life went on. On the other hand, Don's passing hurt deeply. After all he was my long awaited soul mate. The first days after Don died my body and mind lived in numbness. I walked around dazed and barely functioning.Loneliness dominated my life. Yet, I felt relieved suffering and months of heartbreak disappeared. New emotions replaced old ones.

I moved through grief in stages revisiting these stages many times throughout the course of these two years. Anger, depression, guilt, anxiety and sorrow reappeared time and time again. An never ending emotional loop of kept me on the edge of insanity. Chaos ruled in every turn. My family and friends did not understand my anger and frustration. For the first time in my life I could not begin to tell them how I felt. I did not know myself.

Months went by. Still these emotions lingered. Unexpected waves of intense pain, distrust, anger and sadness dominated my emotions while listening to a song, watching movies driving down the highway or looking at his picture. A word, song or thought triggered a profound sadness, one I had never known.

Death affected my physically like not sleeping, lost motivation, and lack of concentration.

Mostly, death was better than living. The world angered me; God did not. Through my experience, I began praying more. Months went by before I read my bible. I sought out another church. I left the church Don, Judy and I attended. I moved to another church, I called my church. I looked for peace.

I avoided places that held memories of Don like Lyons Park, and the pet shop in the mall. About a year later I visited my friend, Mary in the nursing home. His old dining room table, the one we often sat at to play bingo or eat still bothered me. The garden at hospice, and his old rooms at hospice and the VA still bring tears. I tucked his memorial service mementos away from view now along with our wedding albums and cake topper.

It has been two years going into three since he passed. A few weeks ago, I watched a Christian movie showing a grieving family. I cried. I felt their pain. I remembered an incident one week day in April 2010, before Don showed major signs of deterioration. We went to Delbert's house to get dirt. An older lady, dressed in black, stood staring out her window. Her face looked sad. She looked lost. I asked Delbert what was wrong with her, he told me she lost her husband. I remembered thinking how sad. When I lost Don, I understood.

When Don first passed I did not want anyone to be with me for any length of time. I was content alone. I did not have to explain how I felt to anyone when alone. I went to work, support group, church and home. I shopped some, but not excessively.

Life forever changed. Weekends and evenings bother me. I cannot get used to the quiet or not hearing his voice. I work and attend church. I still cry occasionally especially when our anniversary comes around, I think about his birthday or the anniversary of his death.

Last forever however it changed to a different phase. Everyday gets easier with the passage of time although it still hurts. Spiritually this experience made me stronger by striving to meet God's expectations. It is hard. Nothing worth fighting for is easy. Smiles come easier when thinking of special moments, songs or viewing snapshots. Thinking of Don's love reminds me of the sun's warm rays and God's forgiveness.

I wrote:

> I was placed on this world to do good in some capacity. God is now and will always take care of me even though I cannot see Him. I am better for loving Don than without him. He

showed me how to love and be loved which I will never forget. I am sure I will be okay in time. Death is not final, but the beginning. Life is too short to waste it foolishly. I am blessed.

November 1, 2010 during our grief support group meeting at Davis Hospice.

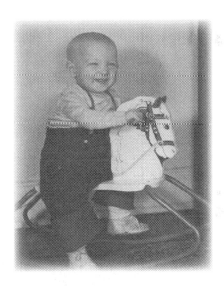

Infant Don

Afterword

I thought about my life—before Don, while he lived and after his journey home. I am certain, my life changed for the better. I am also certain, I will never be the same. No one can ever tell you what you feel or how to feel it. Grief is personal. Delbert once told me with a big smile, "It is not all right but it will be all right." He was right. It was not all right as I struggled daily trying to deal with my feelings and deep sense of loss. It is all right now. Yes, I cried as I thought about the day he passed. I cried as I typed each word. That was hard because each part of the day was as fresh as if it were yesterday.

Just the other day, a friend and fellow widow, Bonnie, invited me to her home for dinner. Bonnie and I went to the memorial services, and grief support groups. We smiled, and talked. We talked about our husbands and how we were doing. We smiled. Grief changed both our lives. We are living now not just surviving. Life is good.

While going through the toughest part of grief, I learned so much. I want to share my lessons. You may agree with some of these thoughts while discarding others. At any rate, I hope you will find what works.

- Hold on to God and do not let go.

- Lean on God, pray without ceasing and read your Bible daily if only a verse.
- Remember God knows how we feel, he lost his only Son to death.
- Take time to forgive.
- Do not cling to material items, they disappear.
- Grief takes lots of energy.
- No one can tell you how to grieve. You have to do it your way.
- Don't try to live up to anyone's expectations of you.
- Be free to change and adapt your life to fit God's expectations of you; not society's
- Take time to reevaluate your life especially your spirituality.
- Find happiness in little moments.
- It's all right to feel sad, loneliness, relief, anger, and guilt.
- Give yourself time to grieve. You cannot rush the process.
- We grieve according to importance of the person who passed.
- Take time to tell people in your life you love them.
- Celebrate their life by creating new traditions.
- You are not defined by your loss.
- Grief causes us to reassess life.
- It's okay not to celebrate holidays.

- Remember their death your way.
- Thinking of holidays are usually worse than the holiday.
- It is all right to wear items belonging to your loved one.
- Keep as many pictures and mementos around as you like.
- Death changes relationships.
- Death may bring greed. People get what they think they deserve.
- Loved ones make promises before they die. Sometimes the person left behind cannot carry out those promises.
- Grieving takes time. It does not stop in a day.
- Grief leaves a hole in the heart that mends over time.
- No one fully understands what you are going through, though they may have lost someone.
- You may have to break traditions. Old ways may not suffice.
- Grief changes a person's outlook on life.
- Friends mean well; but you have to find what suits you.
- What was good then does not necessarily apply now.
- Take time to live. Time is short.
- Talk, talk, talk when ready.
- Try not dwell on the past. Look forward to the future.

- Cherish moments with your loved one. Be grateful for them.
- Try finding hobbies or some activity to help fill the void.
- Journal your thoughts, it helps.
- Look for opportunities to help others
- Focus on positive ways to deal with grief not negative ways.
- Do not give up.
- Give your heart again when ready.
- Finally God's grace is sufficient.

Conclusion

Don's story was about love found and lost, faith and God's grace and mercy. It is also about losing faith in the midst of a crisis only to discover it again later.

When I started writing this story about eight months ago, I found I began healing. Sometimes, parts of the book made me cry while other times I thought of happy memories. Don was the kind of man people gravitated toward. His gentle spirit, kindness and belief in God helped shaped Don as he grew older.

As I traveled through his life, I found he, like all of us, had many faults. Yet, he kept trying. He never gave up at anything he tried. When he quit a job he found a new one. This determination and love of life helped me during the roughest time in my life.

We laughed, cried and prayed together. We lived life to the full and enjoyed most every minute.

Then cancer struck. Suddenly life was not the same. We faced a new challenge that made us look at ourselves, God and our world. Our little space became a place of unrealized hopes and dreams.

Our plans changed moment by moment. I found we created plans by moments. The next moment these plans, we placed so much effort in, changed. I patiently learned moments are plans in the making. We do not get a second chance. Once the moment vanished so do those plans. Then new ones began.

Through all of this experience, God's purpose won over our own. So, life changed and we changed as well.

In the end, he changed again as he readied himself for his final journey—the one towards Heaven. As I looked back into his and my life, I realized this was exactly how our lives were supposed to end. They interconnected exactly at the right moment, not too early or too late.

God's timing is always perfect. I had always heard, God never puts on a person, more than they can bear. I found out this is not in his Word. However, what I discovered was several things about God. First, He loves me more than Don did. God's love is perfect. God does not hold sins against us. He forgets and forgives. Second, God understands our lives because he made us. Third, nothing can ever separate me and God. Finally, God is perfect and I am not. Even though I did trust Him or pray as I should have, he never left me.

Since, Don's death, I pray more and I am learning to trust God. I look forward to hearing him tell me well-done. I still struggle with sin as we all do, however I know it is forgiven. I opened my heart to a Christian, sincere and loving man named Ken, whom I met at my new church Fellowship Baptist. I was and am amazed at God's love and plan for my life.

As I thought about our lives, many scriptures whirled in my head. However the ones I placed in the chapters pertained to life and circumstances. I hope these will help you along your journey.

About the Author

D.K. was employed as a nursing assistant by several medical facilities since seventeen. During a span of about fifteen years she experienced many facets of nursing care. The most impactful was the five years she spent in Oncology and Hospice. These experiences helped her relate to cancer. She saw many types of cancer and many families in that time. As a nursing assistant she spent much time with patients and families. Finally, going through pancreatic cancer with Don gave her another perspective of death and cancer. In addition, year of grief support enabled her to draw fresh conclusions about grief.

She received her Associate of Science in Criminal Justice in May 2008 with honors. August 2009, she graduated with a Bachelor of Science in Criminal Justice, Cum Laude. November 2012, D.K. received a Master of Arts in Education. Currently she is employed as a substitute teacher. She served over twenty-two years in the military.

Outside interests include teaching Sunday school and collaborating on other projects. She has three adult sons, several grandchildren and three adorable cats. D.K. makes her home in Cheyenne, Wyoming.

Time Line

July 3, 1946 Robert Heichel married Dorothy Farst.

May 7, 1947 Don was born.

1950 Vietnam started three years before Don was born.

May 15, 1965 Don received his service number. He was proud of his card.

June 1965 Don graduated from Clear Forks High School, Belville, Ohio.

May 1967 Don formally joined the Army.

May 1968 The Army discharged Don and he returns home.

January 10, 1970 Don married Judy Number One.

September 5, 1971 Robbie was born.

July 11, 1972 Jim was born.

May 17, 1976 Don graduated from the Police academy.

May 19, 1976 Don graduated from Basic Law Enforcement Training.

April 1979 He accepted the position as Butler Police Chief.

November 1979 Don resigned as chief.

July 11, 1980 Judy and Don divorced.

May 15, 1982 Don and Alverna married.

September 15, 1982 Don and Alverna divorced.

October 7, 1983 Don married Judy Number Two.

1990 Don was diagnosed with colon cancer.

1991 He was cancer free.

January 2003 Doctors replaced his left hip with a prosthetic.

August 2007 Don began living in the VA long term facility.

2007 Judy Number Two left him.

March 2008 Don met me.

February 2009 His divorce became final from Judy Number Two.

March 2009 Doctors diagnosed pancreatic cancer.

April 2009 Don and I married.

May 2010 Don began home hospice.

June 2010 Don went to Davis Hospice.

August 3, 2010 He passed away.

Appendix

Chapter 1

Romans 8:26 Likewise the Spirit also helpeth our infirmities: for we know not what we should pray for as we ought: but the Spirit itself maketh intercession for us with groanings which cannot be uttered.

Proverbs 19:21There are many devices in a man's heart; nevertheless the counsel of the LORD, that shall stand.

Chapter 2

Ecclesiastes 3:8 A time to love, and a time to hate; a time of war, and a time of peace

Psalm 25:12 What man is he that feareth the LORD? him shall he teach in the way that he shall choose.

Chapter 3

Ephesians 5:25 Husbands, love your wives, even as Christ also loved the church, and gave himself for it;

1Corinthians 7:10-11 And unto the married I command, yet not I, but the Lord, Let not the wife depart from her husband: But and if she depart, let her remain unmarried or be reconciled to her husband: and let not the husband put away his wife.

Chapter 4

Romans 13:1 Let every soul be subject unto the higher powers. For there is no power but of God: the powers that be are ordained of God.

Chapter 5

Ruth 1:16 And Ruth said, Intreat me not to leave thee, or to return from following after thee: for whither thou goest, I will go; and where thou lodgest, I will lodge: thy people shall be my people, and thy God my God:

Chapter 6

Psalm 73:26 My flesh and my heart faileth: but God is the strength of my heart, and my portion for ever.

Chapter 7

Matthew 12:25 And Jesus knew their thoughts, and said unto them, Every kingdom divided against itself is brought to desolation; and every city or house divided against itself shall not stand:

Chapter 8

Hebrews11:1 Now faith is the substance of things hoped for, the evidence of things not seen.

Chapter 9

Ecclesiastes 4:10 For if they fall, the one will lift up his fellow: but woe to him that is alone when he falleth; for he hath not another to help him up.

Chapter 10

Philippians 2:2 Fulfil ye my joy, that ye be likeminded, having the same love, being of one accord, of one mind.

Chapter 11

Psalm 5:1 Give ear to my words, O LORD, consider my meditation.

2 Corinthians 1:2-4 Blessed be the God and Father of our Lord Jesus Christ, the Father of mercies and God of all comfort, who comforts us in all our tribulation, that we may be able to comfort those who are in any trouble, with the comfort with which we ourselves are comforted by God.

Chapter 12

1 Corinthians 13:4-9Charity suffereth long, and is kind; charity envieth not; charity vaunteth not itself, is not puffed up, Doth not behave itself unseemly, seeketh not her own, is not easily provoked, thinketh no evil; Rejoiceth not in iniquity, but rejoiceth in the truth; Beareth all things, believeth all things, hopeth all things, endureth all things. Charity never faileth: but whether there be prophecies, they shall fail; whether

there be tongues, they shall cease; whether there be knowledge, it shall vanish away For we know in part, and we prophesy in part.

Chapter 13

Ephesians 5:22 Wives, submit yourselves unto your own husbands, as unto the Lord.

Chapter 14

Psalm 25:18 Look upon mine affliction and my pain; and forgive all my sins.

Psalm 40:12-13 For innumerable evils have compassed me about: mine iniquities have taken hold upon me, so that I am not able to look up; they are more than the hairs of mine head: therefore my heart faileth me. Be pleased, O LORD, to deliver me: O LORD, make haste to help me.

Chapter 15

Psalm 27:13 I had fainted, unless I had believed to see the goodness of the LORD in the land of the living.

Chapter 16

Psalm 23:4 Yea, though I walk through the valley of the shadow of death, I will fear no evil: for thou art with me; thy rod and thy staff they comfort me.

Chapter 17

Psalm 89:47Remember how short my time is: wherefore hast thou made all men in vain?

Chapter 18

Psalm 90:12 So teach us to number our days, that we may apply our hearts unto wisdom.

Chapter 19

Psalm 89:4 What man is he that liveth, and shall not see death? shall he deliver his soul from the hand of the grave? Selah.

Chapter 20

Psalm 49:1 For when he dieth he shall carry nothing away: his glory shall not descend after him.

Afterword

Philippians 4:7 And the peace of God, which passeth all understanding, shall keep your hearts and minds through Christ Jesus.

Notes

Chapter 1

1. Romans 8:26 (KJV). The Spirit intercedes for us because we do not know what we are supposed to pray for. Paul writes in Again in Romans 8:27 the Spirit searches our hearts and knows the heart of the Spirit because he makes an intercession to God for the saints according to the will of God.

2. Proverbs 16:9 (KJV) tells us this: a man's heart wants to do what it wants to do but the Lord directs our steps in other words it is God's call to where we should go.

3. Job 1:21 (KJV) said he came into this world without anything as we will die without anything. That is how we die—we do not take anything from this world with us.

4. Matthew 6:20-21 (KJV) We should not live to have anything on this earth. If we place our hearts into what we have on earth, then our hearts will be far from God. Our things on earth go away, however our life in with God is eternal.

Chapter 2

5. Heichel family genealogy, Ancestry.Com, assessed 2011, http://freepages.genealogy.rootsweb.ancestry.com/~fowler/combined/fam07494.htm
6. 1947 Remember When, Seek Publishing
7. Vietnam Timeline, Illinois Edu, accessed November 11, 2011, http://www.english.Illinois/maps/vietnam/timeline.htm

Chapter 3

8. Matthew 5:31-32 (KJV)God meant for us to remain married according to, however we do not always remain married for different reasons.

Chapter 5

9. Baker's asthma is a form of asthma occurring from occupational exposure to flour. Baker's Asthma, Occupational and Environmental Medicine, accessed 2011, http://oem.bmj.com/content/59/7/498.extract.

Chapter 6

10. Psalm 46:11(KJV) says God is with us. He is always by our side no matter what we do.
11. 1 Corinthians 1:9(KJV) .tell us God is faithful, by whom ye were called unto the fellowship of his Son Jesus Christ our Lord. We never have to worry.
12. Matthew 17:20 and Luke 17:6 (KJV) The Lord says if we have faith of a mustard seed we can move mountains.

13. Colon cancer statistics from Colon Cancer survival rates. Colon Cancer, American Cancer Society, accessed 2011, http://www.cancer.org/Cancer/ColonandRectumCancer

14. Colostomy is a procedure where surgeons make a hole in the stomach area so feces excretes from the intestines to the outside using a bag to catch the fecal matter. Colostomy, medical dictionary, accessed 2011, http://medical-dictionary.thefreedictionary.com/Colostomy

15. Medical information used came from a summary of Don's VA treatment from 2003 to 2007

16. Lucent zone is the space between the hip prosthetic and the bone. Don had a cemented device. Problems developed when this zone widened which caused his hip to dislocate. Lucent Zone, Radiology assistant, accessed 2011, http://www.radiologyassistant.nl/en/431c8258e7ac3

17. MRI: Magnetic Resonance imaging may be performed to look at any part of the body. These x-rays are done with or without contrast. This means radiologists give patients a substance to drink that makes the x-ray show more than it would otherwise. MRI, WebMD, accessed 2011, http://www.webmd.com/a-to-z-guides/magnetic-resonance-imaging-mri

18. Bursitis is the space between tendons, joints, muscles and our skin. Bursa sacs help our body move without pain. Bursa sacs, Public Health, accessed 2011, http://www.ncbi.nlm.nih.gov/pubmedhealth/PMH0001456/

19. Rheumatology is the study of arthritis. Arthritis is a disease of the joints but it can also attack the immune system. Arthritis, Rheumatoid Arthritis, accessed 2011, http://www.rheumatoidarthritis.com/ra/understanding-ra/signs-and-symptoms.htm

20. CAT Scan is a computerized Axial tomography image. The scans use x-rays, three dimensional pictures and cross sectional angles form a complete picture. They give doctors a better view than regular x-rays. CAT Scans, Medicine net, accessed 2011, http://www.medicinenet.com/cat_scan/article.htm

21. Staph is a germ patients get. It is very hurtful if it gets into the body like bones, and joints. Treatment is antibiotics. , Staph, Mayo Clinic, accessed 2011, http://www.mayoclinic.com/health

22. Aspirate: is taking fluid from an area by needle or tube. Aspirate, EHow, accessed 2011, http://www.ehow.com/way_5791900_procedure-hip-joint-after-surgery.html

23. Sepsis is an infection caused by bacteria that travels throughout the blood stream. Sepsis, Medical Terms, accessed 2011, http://www.medterms.com/script/main/art.asp?articlekey=5449

24. A centimeter is a unit of measurement used in science, medicine and other disciplines. One centimeter equals 0.393700787 inches.

25. Debridment is removal dead tissue by surgery. Debridment, Merriam Webster Dictionary, accessed 2011, http://www.merriam-webster.com/dictionary/debridement

26. Spacer this is a device impregnated with an antibiotic to help patients with infection. Use of these spacers usually gets rid of infection in patients with hip or knew replacements. http://www.medicalnewstoday.com/releases/144908.php

27. 1 Corinthians 3:12 (KJV) Rewards are what we get in Heaven. There are four—gold, precious stones, hay, wood or stubble. Mark 1:4, Luke 3:13, Luke 24:47, Acts 2:38 and Acts 3:19 (KJV) Repent is a new mind set. According to the Bible when we accept Christ as our Lord (become a Christian) we do not continue doing the same sins as before. Our minds are renewed. These scriptures tell us that repenting is part of the process of salvation.

Chapter 7

28. Romans 5:3-5 (KJV) When we persevere through trials, we get stronger. God tells us in that perseverance brings hope. And not only so, but we glory in tribulations also: knowing that tribulation worketh patience; And patience, experience; and experience, hope: And hope maketh not ashamed; because the love of God is shed abroad in our hearts by the Holy Ghost which is given unto us.

29. Job 1-42 God gave the devil permission to take everything from Job except his life. In the end, God gave Job everything back and more. The book of Job is a powerful book because it showed Job's devotion to God no matter the circumstances.

Chapter 8

30. Proverbs 16:33(KJV) We choose activities and events however, God it is up to the Lord "The lot is cast into the lap; but the whole disposing thereof is of the LORD."

Chapter 9

31. 1John 1:9 (KJV The following scriptures describe God's process for eternal life. We want this above all else because everything on earth passes away. In that all of us will die. Confessing sins-): If we confess our sins, he is faithful and just to forgive our sins and to cleanse us from all righteousness. 1 John 2:15 (KJV) man love the world, the love of the Father is not in him. For all that is in the world, the lust of the flesh, and the lust of the eyes, and the pride of life, is not of the Father, but is of the world. And the world passeth away, and the lust thereof, but he that doeth the will of God abideth for ever. Acts 2:21(KJV):And it shall come to pass, that whosoever shall call on the name of the Lord shall be saved. Obey-Matthew 28:19-20(KJV): Go ye therefore, and teach all nations, baptizing them in the name of the Father, and of the Son, and of the Holy Ghost; teaching them to observe all things whatsoever I have commanded you: and lo, I am with you always, even unto the end of the world. These are powerful statements that we should not do what the world expects but what God expects us to do.

32. Frontier Days is a week-long celebration in Cheyenne during the last couple of weeks in July. Many activities tell of the western days in Cheyenne.

Chapter 10

33. Proverbs 21:2 Every way of a man is right in his own eyes: but the LORD pondereth the hearts. Humans look at a person's outside appearance and what they portray. God looks at the heart. I may see sincere qualities but I have no way of judging what is in the person's heart.

Chapter 11

34. Psalm 54:2(KJV) says "Hear my prayer, O God; give ear to the words of my mouth." God wants us to pray not with idle words but with sincere hearts. God listens to prayer
35. Titus 2:3-44(KJV):That they may teach the young women to be sober, to love their husbands, to love their children, To be discreet, chaste, keepers at home, good, obedient to their own husbands, that the word of God be not blasphemed.
36. Upper GI or gastrointestinal tract consists of the esophagus, stomach and small intestine. Digestive diseases, National Digestive Diseases Information Clearing house, accessed 2011, http://digestive. niddk.nih.gov/ddiseases/pubs/uppergi/#1

Chapter 13

37. Whipple procedure: This procedure treats some patients with pancreatic cancer. It is a very extensive surgery removing the pancreatic head, bile duct and part of the small intestine. Pancreatic Diseases, University of Southern California, accessed 2011, http://www.surgery.usc.edu/divisions/tumor/pancreasdiseases/web%20pages/pancreas%20resection/whipple%20operation.html

Chapter 14

38. (Bilary)stent placement: An instrument called an endoscope helps doctors place these small stents in the biliary tubes which opens them allowing bile to flow. Bilary Stent, Surgery Enclopedia, , accessed 2011, http://www.surgeryencyclopedia.com/A-Ce/Biliary-Stenting.html

Chapter 15

39. Endoscope: an instrument with a lighted end. Endoscope, Medical News Today, accessed 2011, http://www.medicalnewstoday.com/articles/153737.php
40. These are different levels of cancer. Pancreatic stages, University of Maryland, Greenebaum Cancer Center, accessed 2011, http://www.umgcc.org/gi_program/pan-stages.htm
41. Pancreatic cancer survival rate is the amount of patients living at least five years with this cancer. Only one percent survival rates for stage

four according to the American Cancer Society. Pancreatic Survival rates, American Cancer Society, accessed 2011, http://www.cancer.org/Cancer/PancreaticCancer/DetailedGuide/pancreatic-cancer-survival-rates

Chapter 16

42. Chemotherapy medications: strong medications given during the cancer treatment. Regimesnts depend on the type of cancer and patient needs. Chemotherapy, ChemoCare, accessed 2011, http://www.chemocare.com/bio/

43. Neutropenic is when cancer drugs cannot tell good cells from cancer cells. Thus white blood counts decrease. Neutropenia, Neulasta, accessed 2011, http://www.neulasta.com/paticnt/about/about-low-white-blood-cell-count.html?src=ppc&WT.srch=1&SRC=2

Chapter 17

44. Stages of dying: each patient may go through different points of the dying process before death. Stages of Dying, University of Kentucky, accessed 2011, http://www.uky.edu/~cperring/kr.htm

45. Mark 7:21-23(KJV) For from within, out of the heart of men, proceed evil thoughts, adulteries, fornications, murders, Thefts, covetousness, wickedness, deceit, lasciviousncss, an evil eye, blasphemy, pride, foolishness: All these evil things come from within, and defile the man. The Bible

has many scriptures relating to pride these are several. 1Timothy 1:6(KJV) Not a novice, lest being lifted up with pride he fall into the condemnation of the devil. 1 John 2:16(KJV) For all that is in the world, the lust of the flesh, and the lust of the eyes, and the pride of life, is not of the Father, but is of the world.

Chapter 18

46. Jesus death is significant because he died for our sins where no one else had. He loved us more than our spouses, children, parents or friends. John 3:16 (KJV)For God so loved the world, that he gave his only begotten Son, that whosoever believeth in him should not perish, but have everlasting life. Hebrews 12:9 (KJV)But we see Jesus, who was made a little lower than the angels for the suffering of death, crowned with glory and honour; that he by the grace of God should taste death for every man.

47. Matthew 6:14, Ephesians 4:32 and Luke 6:37 talk about forgiveness.

Glossary

ACT/SAT— College entrance exams

Aspirate— Removal of fluid from the body

Baker's asthma— A form of asthma occurring from exposure to flour dust

Bursitis— Inflammation around the bursa are fluid filled sacs that help the body to move without rubbing

Cc— A type of measurement used mostly used in sciences like medicine

Colon cancer—When cells mutate inside the intestinal wall

CAT scan—A computerized X-ray called Computerized Axial Tomography is another type of X-Ray

Chemotherapy—A type of treatment for different types of cancers

Dexamethasone Sodium Phosphate—A type of chemotherapy drug

Endoscope—An instrument with a light on it used for looking inside the body

Eosinophilia cells—A type of cells in the blood

Femoral Stem—A part of the hip replacement device connecting the artificial joint to the hip

Gastrointestinal—Stomach and intestines

Lucent zone—Area around the hip replacement device

MRI— Another type of X-Ray, Magnetic Resonance Images use magnetic pulses to take pictures of the body.

Ondansetron— A kind of chemotherapy drug to combat cancer. It can be used with other drugs

Pancreatic cancer— Abnormal cell mutations in the pancreas that sometimes involves the liver, stomach and surrounding organs.

Pancreas— A small organ that helps regulate the digestive system

Percocet—A narcotic drug prescribed by licensed medical personnel

Predisone dosepak—A steroid that may help decrease swelling and other symptoms. Dosepaks allow patients to start with high doses then tapers down to lower dosages

Prochlorperazine Maleate—Another drug used in chemotherapy

Rheumatology—The study of arthritis

Staph—Bacteria that may travel throughout the body

Videorama—A kind of television in the 1940s

Resources

Cancer and cancer support

http://www.cancer.org/

http://www.pancreaticalliance.org/panca/support.html

Grief and grief support

http://www.onlinegriefsupport.com/

http://www.dailystrength.org/c/Bereavement/support-group

Hospice

http://hospicenet.org/

http://www.hospicefoundation.org/

Lung Disease

http://www.lung.org/

http://www.nationaljewish.org/

Marriage

http://fireproofmymarriage.com/

http://www.daily-devotionals.com/tag/fireproof-your-marriage-what-are-the-40-steps/

Scriptures

The King James Version Public Domain

http://www.biblegateway.com/